Thomas Griffith

From Sin to Salvation

The Pauline Picture of the Redemptive Process

Thomas Griffith

From Sin to Salvation
The Pauline Picture of the Redemptive Process

ISBN/EAN: 9783744665506

Printed in Europe, USA, Canada, Australia, Japan

Cover: Foto ©Lupo / pixelio.de

More available books at **www.hansebooks.com**

From Sin to Salvation.

THE PAULINE PICTURE OF THE REDEMPTIVE PROCESS.

BY

THOMAS GRIFFITH, A.M.,

LATE PREBENDARY OF ST. PAUL'S.

London:
HODDER AND STOUGHTON,
27, PATERNOSTER ROW.

MDCCCLXXXII.

"*If life be worth living, it is so only when we live it ourselves, and help others to live it, in a manner worthy of life.*"—LACTANTIUS.

"*He too is doing a soldier's work who, though withdrawn from the line of battle, stands sentry at the gates, and looks after the military stores.*"—SENECA.

CONTENTS.

CHAP.		PAGE
I.	INTRODUCTORY	3
II.	SECURITY UNDER SIN	43
III.	STRUGGLE AGAINST SIN	61
IV.	SLAVERY TO SIN	79
V.	SUFFERING FROM SIN	95
VI.	HOPE OF RIGHTEOUSNESS	107
VII.	FREEDOM FOR RIGHTEOUSNESS	125
VIII.	LIFE FOR RIGHTEOUSNESS	139
IX.	POWER FOR RIGHTEOUSNESS	165

CHAPTER I.

INTRODUCTORY.

I.

ONE cannot open Milton's "Paradise Regained" without being surprised at the entirely different theory it gives of the redemptive work of Christ from that put forth in the "Paradise Lost." In the earlier poem we have the Calvinistic doctrine of salvation by the vicarious sufferings of Jesus; in the later, the rationalistic doctrine of salvation by the personal sanctity of Jesus. In the first all is summed up in—

> "Die man or justice must, unless for him
> Some other, able and as willing, pay
> The rigid satisfaction, *death for death*."

But in the second, the one note sounded from first to last is—

> "Recovered Paradise to all mankind,
> By one man's firm *obedience*, fully tried
> Through all temptation, and the tempter foiled."

And some divines have fallen into this mistake; erecting thereon a whole system of theology, which makes the sanctity of Jesus, and our imitation of it, do duty for his sufferings and our salvation through them. But the text on which they mainly rely (Heb. x. 7-10), speaks manifestly, not of doing God's will in *general*, by a holy life; but doing that *particular* will which demanded a vicarious death. For the Son says, "Lo, I come to do *that will* by which we are sanctified *through the offering* of the body of Jesus Christ;" to supersede by the sacrifice of myself the sacrifices offered by the law. Or, as St. Paul has put it in Phil. ii. 8, "he became obedient" (*i.e.*, submissive) "unto *death*, even death upon the cross." Just as in Heb. ii. 9 the reason given for the Incarnation is not that Jesus might live as our example, but that he might die as our substitute,—"he was made lower than the angels *for the suffering of death;* that he might *taste death for every man.*"

But Milton, in both these entirely opposite

views of the redemptive work of Christ, as well as the divines on both sides who share these views, has overlooked the one distinctive feature of this work which pervades the writings of John and Paul; its turning essentially, not simply on the vicarious sufferings nor on the personal sanctity of Jesus (these are but preparatives, means to a further end), but on his *resurrection life*, when he ascended into the heavens, there to live with God and unto God; there to receive gifts for men; and thence to send down, as his representative and his abiding Presence, that "Spirit of Christ," that "Spirit of him who raised up Christ from the dead," who should become to all his people "the Giver of *life;*" the perennial source of all faith, all love, all hope, all power. *This* it is emphatically which marks out Christianity as *the* saving dispensation. *This*, to which the prophets pointed, and which Jesus promised, as the one glory of the Messianic age. *This*, therefore, which should form the central point of every Christian system of divinity. We have had specially purchased for us *the Spirit* of Christ; we have had engaged to us this Spirit; we are heirs of this Spirit; we are living under what is distinctively the dispensation of this Spirit: and only therefore as we drink copiously of its regenerating streams can we experience the redemptive work of Christ. Without this Spirit all is sin and sorrow. With this Spirit all is sanctity and joy. And the contrast between the two positions is nothing short of the contrast between darkness and light, between death and life.

And yet the baneful habit of interpreting Scripture, not by the clear light of the writer's position, purpose, and line of argument, but by the dim suggestions of our own personal experience, has led many students of that section of the Epistle to the Romans, in which the Apostle Paul points out this striking contrast with the boldest outline and the most distinctive colours, to blur this clear outline and dilute these contrasted colours into a weakened wash of neutral tint.

We must therefore begin our exposition of this passage with the avowal that we find ourselves compelled, by all the laws of grammatico-historical interpretation, and by the whole tenor and texture of the apostle's graduated chart of his own transition from sin to salvation, to contemplate this real though highly coloured picture as a delineation of (first) the helpless condition of every moralist without the Spirit of Christ; and (next) the totally opposite condition to which such a seeker after righteousness becomes exalted by the infusion into him of this Spirit. That this is the purpose of St. Paul is shown very early in the section by his saying (vii. 5), "When we *were* in the flesh" (*i.e.*, still denizens of this lower world) "the impulses of sin which the law did but aggravate wrought in our members to bring upon us death;" which is plainly the description of a stage from which the apostle has passed away, at the time he is writing; in perfect *contrast* with the stage which he describes in the very next sentence as the present one of himself and all true

Christians: "But *now* we have been freed from the law, to serve God with all the spontaneity of a new-born spirit in a new sphere of life." And then the plural "we" slides into the more emphatic singular "I," to indicate that Paul is delineating his own experience in the matter as a representative portrait of all who *were* once in the bondage of the flesh, but are *now* rejoicing in the freedom of the spirit. And the logical necessity for so interpreting this section is as great as the grammatical. For, as Professor Godwin has pithily put it in a single sentence, "The whole of this description is to show the powerlessness of the Law in contrast to the power of the Gospel; therefore to suppose that Christian experience is described in the seventh chapter is to make the argument of the apostle *self-destructive*, seeing that thus the *inefficacy of the Gospel* would be proved as well as that of the Law."* This too is the view of all the Greek Fathers up to the time of Augustine; nay of Augustine himself, till his judgment

---

* "Godwin on the Romans," 185.

became warped by his contest with Pelagius, and he merged the calm expositor in the heated controversialist. For on Rom. vii. 19 he had written, "Now is there described a man under law, *before grace;*" and on vii. 25, "*Henceforth* Paul begins to describe a man *under grace.*"

And to this view, all the apostle had said before leads up. For in the fifth chapter he strikes the key-note of the whole section when he says (verse 21), "As sin has reigned to bring men down to death, so shall grace reign through righteousness, to bring them up to life, through Jesus Christ our Lord." Then, in the sixth chapter, he meets the unhallowed suggestion of self-indulgence, "Shall we not, then, continue sinning, and thus make more conspicuous the freeness of this grace?" by asserting the entire transition of every truly regenerate person from the very atmosphere of sin into the atmosphere of righteousness alone. For (he argues) as surely as our Master, dying on the cross, bade farewell to this sinful world, to pass on into that region of purity where the Father dwells, so surely every one baptized into the participation of this death of Jesus has pledged himself thereby to pass away from the servitude of sin into that totally opposite service of God, of which the fruit is holiness and the final harvest is eternal life (vi. 21-33). And it is expressly to illustrate, and bring out clear before the eyes of every one, the completeness of this transition to which the Christian is pledged by his baptism, that Paul then adds the seventh and eighth chapters. He shows how the Law itself supplies an image of the new condition of freedom into which the Christian is transferred by his participation in the death of Jesus. And he confirms this by a vivid picture of his own experience in passing from a hopeless struggle with sin and guilt into the blessed calm of peace with God, and living unto God, which is produced by the Spirit of our risen Lord.

This, then, is the passage which we must read through and study well.

ROMANS VII. 1 to VIII. 17.

CHAPTER VII.

"You cannot be ignorant, brethren, (for I am writing to men who are well acquainted with the law of Moses,) that this Law has lordship over any one, only during the life of its subjects. A woman (for instance), who is bound by the Law to her husband, becomes released from this bond as soon as the husband dies. And, therefore, though during her husband's lifetime she would have been considered an adulteress had she given herself to any other man, when the husband dies she is loosed from her obligations to him, and contracts no stain of adultery though she marry another man. Now just in like manner ye also, brethren, have become, like that husband, dead to the Law,

through your identification with the dying Christ, in order that, like the widowed wife, you may lawfully be married to another (I mean to the risen Christ), to bring forth offspring to
5 God.* When indeed you were still alive in the body, the impulses of Sin, multiplied by the restrictions of the Law, begat in you results whose penalty
6 is Death; but now that we have figuratively become dead to the body, we

* Here is a double comparison; first to the dying husband, like whom the Christian dies, as it were with his dying Lord; and next, to the surviving wife, like whom the Christian also continues alive with his living Lord, wedded to him for the bringing forth of children (*i.e.*, good works) to God. This *death*, with Christ, to sin, is well described by M. Olier, as "un état où le cœur ne peut être ému en son fond ; et, quoique le monde lui montre ses beautés, ses honneurs, ses richesses, c'est tout de même comme s'il les offrait à un mort, qui demeure insensible à tout ce qui se presente" (cf. Gal. vi. 14). And the *life* into which the Christian rises, with Christ, may be defined, in the words of Emerson, "a rise, as by specific levity, not into a particular virtue, but into *the region of all the virtues.*"

have become as much emancipated from the Law as if we had literally died out of its jurisdiction; and henceforth, therefore, we may serve God in that new way which the Spirit prompts, instead of the old way which the letter prescribed.*

But † do I mean when I declared the 7

---

* The reference here is plainly to the prophetic promise in Jer. xxxi. 33, "I will make a new covenant with the house of Israel, putting my law into their inward parts, so that no longer need men teach their neighbours to know the Lord, for all shall know him, from the least to the greatest," which St. John also regards as fulfilled in Christians, when he tells them, "Ye need no teaching from any one, for the anointing of the Spirit teaches you concerning all things." The difference here commemorated is just that pointed out by Xenocrates, when he said that his disciples "came to do of their own will what the laws had bound upon them." Only Paul, like Jesus, goes beyond this; from the narrow precepts of a defunct law to the all-embracing principles of a living Spirit.

† Paul feels that his previous assertion (5) that sins were multiplied by Law (cf. v. 20) would be resented as a slander on the Law. He therefore breaks off here into a long digression (7 to 24) to put the blame on our inbred corruption. This it is which not only checks

impulses of Sin to be multiplied under the Law, to decry the Law itself as sinful? Far from me such a thought! On the contrary, I acknowledge the Law as having first disclosed to me Sin. For I should have had no consciousness (for instance) of my being covetous, unless the Law had commanded,
8 Thou shalt not covet. What, then, I mean is this; that Sin, taking advantage of this commandment, stirred up in me all manner of covetousness. For where no prohibition is pronounced Sin nestles undiscovered, and the sinner
9 has no fear; but as soon as prohibition comes to our hearing, up springs the inbred Sin to life, and the sinner sinks
10 down appalled to death. Thus it was

our endeavours to keep the Law (15 to 17), but dwells in us as the enemy of every good thought (18 to 21); and so drags us down, as its slaves, to death (22 to 24).

that the very commandment which was given to lead me on to Life, I found perverted to bring upon me Death. Because Sin laid hold of the Law, to ¹¹ stir me up to breaking the Law, and thus to expose me to its penalty of Death. You see, then, that I count the ¹² Law itself to be nothing but holy, and its commandments holy and just and good.*

What then? you will ask, this good ¹³ Law, did it bring upon you Death? † No! no! Far from us such a thought! I say again that it was Sin which took advantage of that which was good to work out Death to me, that so, by such perversion of the Law, this Sin

---

* "Holy," of divine origin; "just," of reasonable contents; "good," of beneficent intention.

† Every one knows St. Paul's propensity to go off at a word. He answers at the moment the objection raised by his own phrase, and thus involves reason

might show itself in its blackest form.

14 For while we know well that the Law is spiritual, a model of purity,* this experience disclosed to me how I myself, upon the contrary, am impure and fleshly, the very slave of Sin.

15 The slave, I say, of Sin. For my doings I find clean contrary to my

under reason, like the wheels within wheels of complicated machinery. The involutions in this chapter may be thus tabulated:

1—6. Being dead to the sin-stirring Law we must live now to God.
    7—12. "The sin-stirring Law"? But the Law is holy! Yes; nevertheless it became Death to me through its misuse by Sin.
        13—14. "Became Death to you"? How can the good Law work evil? Because I was enslaved to Sin.
            15—17. "Enslaved to Sin"? Yes; for he had possession of me.
                18—20. "Possession of me"? Yes; for I could not do what I would.

21—24. Thus, then, we return to the original proposition, demonstrated by accumulated proof, that it is *Sin* which through the Law works in us Death.

* "Spiritual" here is the equivalent of "holy, just, and good," in verse 12.

judgment. What I approve, I fail to accomplish; and what I abhor, this very thing I do. But if my judgment thus denies my doings, this shows that I go along with the Law as right, and therefore that it cannot be I (my proper self) who am acting thus, but must be the Sin which has taken possession of me.*

And I say "taken possession of me," for this experience discovers that in myself (that is, my animal nature) good has no place; since just then when I find in me a will for good, I do not

---

* Not I myself, so far as my better nature goes, but sin enslaving this better nature. Paul identifies himself with his *Ideal* in order to disown his *acts;* and thus distinguishes his true permanent self, which responds to right, from his false temporary self, which submits to wrong. And so Fouillée says, " Ce que nous *subissons* doit nous paraître étranger ; or, nous pouvons devenir en quelque sorte *passifs*" (*La Liberté*, 118). And hence the Vedas plead, "It was not our doing, O Varuna ! It was a slip. Even sleep is not free from Sin ! "

therewith find any power for good. ¹⁹ For the good which I purpose I do not perform, and the evil which I purpose ²⁰ not, this is what I do. Surely, then, if I do the very contrary to what I purpose, it cannot be I who have wrought out such doing; it must be Sin which has taken possession of me.*

²¹ See, then (to return now to my former assertion, ver. 14), how true is that which I bewailed—my slavery to Sin. For just then when I am determining to do the graceful thing, then does there start up before me that ²² which is disgraceful. When with my inner nature I go along with the law of ²³ God, I behold in my members another law warring against the law of my mind,

---

* So we read in 1 Chron. xxi. 1: "*Satan* provoked David to number Israel." Yet this did not lessen David's responsibility, for he himself confesses (xxi. 8), "I have *sinned* greatly because *I have done* this thing."

and reducing me into slavery to the law of Sin which dwells in these members.* O miserable man that I am! ²⁴ who is there to free me from this body thus dragging me to Death? Thank ²⁵ God, there is deliverance in Jesus Christ my Lord!

Thus then I have shown how, under the Law, the very same man who in mind is loyal to the law of God, becomes through his body enslaved to the law of Sin.

* Note how, throughout this chapter, there is the assumption of an "inner nature" in the most enslaved man, which constitutes his permanent personality. In the midst of Paul's lowest estimate of man as "flesh," he maintains the highest estimate of man as "mind." So Mr. Hodgson well says, "The discrepancy between the agent's own moral idea and his own act is what his conscience reproaches him with. For the agent identifies himself *with his ideal and not with his act;* and distinguishes his *true* self from his actual but temporary self, so long as he listens to the voice of conscience."—*Mind*, No. xxii. And similarly Dr. Caird: "The form of the finite life is a thing foreign

Chapter VIII.

1 But now,* in contrast with all this (to return to the point whence we digressed in chap. vii. 7), there is no doom of Death impending over those
2 who are in Christ Jesus, because with all who are in him the new law of the Spirit, who leads on to Eternal Life, has set us free from that old law of the letter, under which Sin drives men
3 to death.† For just the very thing

and alien to the true self. Evil, error, imperfection do not really belong to it: they are excrescences, which have no organic relation to the true nature."—*Phil. of Religion*, 299.

* The "now" here takes us back to vii. 6, "*Now* then, through our death and resurrection with Christ having freed us from the jurisdiction and the penalties of the Law." Whence it follows that the sentence of the Law no longer hangs over us. The "no condemnation" in viii. 1 is in antithesis to the "Death" of vii. 24, and the "condemnation" of v. 16, 18.

† "That old law of the letter." For "the Law" in the following verse (3) is manifestly the Law of *Moses*. As manifestly, therefore, its next immediate antecedent

which that old Law could not confer on us, because paralysed by the flesh, this God now bestows on us. Sending His own Son in the likeness of that flesh which in other men causes Sin, and in order to become a sacrifice for Sin, he has inflicted on Christ's flesh the Death demanded by the Law, that 4 he may bestow the Life * promised

here must be the same Law. Besides, Paul could not say of the "Law of the Spirit" in the past tense, "It has set us free from *sin*," since this law of the Spirit only *provides* for freedom, supplies the power for freedom, *on condition* that we breathe its atmosphere and follow its dictates (cf. v. 4, "*if* we walk in the Spirit"). Whereas the Law of the Spirit *has*, once for all, set us free from the obligations of the *Law of Moses* (cf. Gal. v. 18, "If ye be led by the Spirit you are no longer in subjection to the Law of Moses"). To call this Law of Moses one " of sin and death," is no more than Paul had already done in vii. 5: "The motions of Sin, intensified by the Law, brought forth fruit unto Death." And he does so again in 1 Cor. xv. 56,—" Sin derives its strength from the Law;" and in 2 Cor. iii. 6, 9, " The letter killeth ;" and " Moses is the minister of condemnation."

* Dikaiōma (right to life) is here opposed to katákrima (condemnation to death) in ver. 1, as in ch. v. 16; and means by the Law on all who live no longer in the atmosphere of flesh, but in that of Spirit.

5   I say "who live no longer in the atmosphere of flesh;" for all who so live become enslaved to fleshly impulses; just as those who breathe the atmosphere of Spirit become actuated 6 by the Spirit's influences.* And slavery to fleshly impulses brings with it, of necessity, Death; while actuation by the Spirit's influences is followed by 7 Life and bliss. Because when enslaved

---

the *blessing* pronounced by the Law, instead of its *curse*. Comp. the parallelism in Psalm xxiv. 5.

  "He shall receive the *blessing* from the Lord,
    And *right to life* from the God of his salvation."

  * To "mind" any thing is to keep it continually in mind, to give ourselves up to it. See the same word in Phil. iii. 19, "They give their whole mind to earthly matters;" and Col. iii. 2, "Give your mind to heavenly principles." Comp. our similar phrases, "given to much wine;" "given up to pleasure," "to ambition," etc.

to fleshly impulses we are in rebellion against God; with neither will nor power to keep the Law of God. Consequently, while we are living under the sway of our lower nature we can never please God.

But ye are no longer under this sway of the lower nature, if the Spirit of God has taken up his abode within you. If, indeed, any one have not this Spirit of Christ, that man is none of his. But if Christ be dwelling in you, then, though still your body must suffer the penalty of Death because of sin, your spirit shall gain the gift of Life because of righteousness.* Nay, more; if the Spirit of him who raised up Christ from the dead be dwelling in

---

* "The *gift* of life," for this is the contrast implied in the term dikaiōma (the promised blessing), and expressed in Rom. vi. 23, "The *wages* of sin is death, but the *gift* of God is eternal life." It may be illustrated by Dr.

you, he who raised up Christ from the dead shall also give life even to your mortal bodies by means of his Spirit dwelling in you.

12 See then, brethren, how indispensable it is that we should live no longer as if embodied persons subject to the
13 sway of flesh. For if you live as subject to the flesh, you are travelling on to Death. Only through slaying this flesh by means of the greater power of the Spirit can you travel on to Life.*

14 Yes! travel on to Life! For all who are actuated by the Spirit of God are

---

Blackie's distinction concerning university prizes: "They should be *not a pecuniary compensation* for intellectual work done, but *an honourable publication* of intellectual facts achieved." Not, therefore, so much Rewards as Awards.

* So Plato declares, "Only by commingling with the divine nature can we ourselves become divine" (Laws, x. 904). And S. Antony, "There is but one way of overcoming our ghostly enemies; namely, by a perpetual bearing of God in our minds."

regarded by him as sons of God. Of 15
this your own experience is a witness.
For what has Christ infused into you?
Not, over again, that spirit of Fear
which once possessed you, but a new
spirit of filial confidence, which cries
aloud to God, "Abba," that is
"Father!" This very spirit, I say, 16
bears witness to our spirit, that we
are children of God. And then it 17
follows, of course, "If children, heirs;
heirs of God as much as Christ
himself is heir!"*

Now when we have studied this close-compacted Section throughout, in its completeness, we shall be struck at once by the two marked *contrasts* it presents—of Sin victorious over Righteousness, and of Righteousness victorious over Sin; of the dispensation of Law ending in

* Cf. 1 Peter iv. 13, "When his glory shall be revealed ye shall glory with him, with exceeding joy."

Death, and the dispensation of Spirit ending in Life. But we shall not be duly prepared to appreciate the full force of these contrasts unless we remember that the first side of them includes the moral history not alone of any one particular man, but of all men on whom the great problem of life has dawned. The portrait is, like all good portraits, an individual *idealized*. And its eyes, like those of all good portraits, look with startling meaning on every beholder. Paul, as a moral wrestler, contending with sin and seeking about for weapons to put down sin, is set before us as a symbol of *human nature at large*, wherever Law has begun to dawn upon it, conscience to be awakened, and the struggle to rise above oneself to be aroused.* It is the glory of man that, among all earthly creatures he only has a conscience; and it is at the same time his shame and grief that this conscience is continually erring, feeble, beaten down by opposing

---

* "L'histoire d'un homme est l'histoire de tous les hommes; une épreuve plus ou moins longue, plus ou moins dangereuse."—ALEX. DUMAS.

influences. At first glance we behold him manly strong and beautiful as the Laocoon; but the next glance shows him to us, like the Laocoon, striving to unwind from himself the filthy folds of the deadly serpent, but striving in vain. And till we fill our minds with the recollection of this state of human nature at large we shall not duly feel the comprehensiveness of St. Paul's whole statement, nor the distinguishing glory of Christ in supplying the only valid solution of a problem which not only Paul and conscientious Jews, but so many in all lands, have laboured at in vain. Only as we bring before us how many have felt themselves under a law higher than that of sense; how many have found in themselves an inbred opposition to this law; how many have groaned under the wretchedness which this opposition entails; and how many have therefore sighed and cried for power beyond their own to effect this deliverance;—only thus shall we estimate what an universal interest attaches to the subject we are about to consider, and how indispensable it is for us to follow Paul throughout his treatment of it, till we reach the height of freedom and of bliss which he attained in Christ.

1. Remember, then, what a universal thing it is for human nature, in its due development, to *find itself under a law higher than that of sense.* It is well said by the son of Sirach that "God, giving men understanding, has *therewith* given them discrimination of good from evil." Whence Cicero declares that "all Law is nothing but that discriminating Reason, derived from the gods themselves, which enjoins upon us all things proper and forbids their contraries." Such Law, therefore, Plato asserts to have been "inscribed upon the tablets of man's heart by God." Of such Law Sophocles says :—

> "It is not of to-day,
> Or yesterday, but through all ages lives,
> And none know whence it springs."

Such law Pindar proclaims to be "Sovereign over all men." Of such law Cicero affirms, "Not by the ingenuity of man has it been thought out, nor by the advanced intelligence of nations decreed; but it is a somewhat ever living; a wisdom concerning right and wrong which dominates the universe. Such law therefore is not merely older than nations and cities, but it is coeval with him who governs the whole heaven and earth. Nay, such law is not simply coeval with the Supreme, it is supreme in the Supreme; and our participation of it and acquiescence in it constitute our similarity to this Supreme. To this our nature is attuned. This has over us a never-dying authority. This summons us to duty by its demands, deters us from sin by its denunciations. No one may abrogate this law, nor take from it one jot or tittle. No senate and no popular vote can loose us from its bonds. No subtle sophist may venture to explain it away. It must be ever its own interpreter. Nor is it one law at Rome, another at Athens; at one time valid, at another not; but over all peoples, throughout all time, does it reign, suffering no death and subject to no change."

And why? Because, as Confucius also maintains, "The law that is inborn in the heart of man is the law of heaven itself; the reason in man is the reason that pervades the universe." The recognition, then, of the divine authority of law, the consenting to law that it is good; the delighting in law after the inward man; the worship of law as holy, just, and good, from which Paul dates his whole experience of the moral life, is shared with him by all enlightened minds. For the Mosaic Law, to which he looked, was but the special exponent, for a particular people, through a passing phase of their education, of the universal will of God.

2. Nor is there less consent of general suffrage with the subsequent experience of St. Paul in regard to the discovery in himself of *an inbred opposition to this law*. Xenophon, for instance, tells us that "man is so self-contradictory that he seems to harbour within him not one soul but two; and when the good one has the upper hand his acts are

graceful, but when the evil one, disgraceful." So also Plato: "In every man there are two leading principles, the one born with us which craves for what is pleasant; the other added after, which looks to what is right. When this last prevails we are submissive to reason, but when the former we are riotous against it." And Euripides complains not only that "there is in every man inborn sin," but also that "when we know full well what is the right thing, nay, and recognize its claims upon us, still we do it not." Whence his Medea confesses, "The very thing I am going to commit I have learned to be wrong, yet my passions overpower my principles." Nay more, the very law itself is complained of (precisely as it is by Paul) as provoking and multiplying transgressions against itself. "Forbidden fruit is the more enticing because of its being forbidden." "We press the more eagerly towards that which is prohibited, and long the more earnestly for that which is denied to us." "Alas!" (exclaims one) "I have neither strength nor authority for ruling myself aright, but am hurried onward in a wrong direction like a vessel in a racing current." "Sin" (declare others) "is therefore a state of slavery." "No one but the righteous man is free!"

3. What wonder then if we find humanity at large, like the once so wretched apostle, *groaning under the misery* which such opposition entails. For herein lie the mingled majesty and misery of man, that while he is following the seemingly strongest laws of his nature he finds himself arraigned and condemned by higher laws, weaker in action but mightier in authority, which go on pertinaciously demanding, even when they cannot achieve, dominion over him. The animals inferior to him follow without reserve their native instincts, with no consciousness, and no imputation, of wrong-doing; nay, rather their very excess of violence, of lust, of audacity, raises them above their fellows and makes them "survivors" in the struggle of

life. But a man, when he gives himself up to similar excess, is felt by others and even by himself to have degraded rather than exalted himself in the scale of worthiness, and to have become not the fortunate victor over weakness, listlessness, and cowardice, but the unhappy victim of inconsistency, reproach, and shame. He has not followed his real nature, but has become distempered from it, as an abscess, an imposthume, a monstrosity in the otherwise well-organized world. "For he" (says Antoninus) "who flies off from the control of the divine reason is a wen, an abscess, in the universe." "His rage, his avarice, his envy" (declares another) "show that there is no health in him." Nay, he is not pitiable simply, he is condemnable, as rebellious against the law within him, and the lawgiver above him. "He is a traitor to his own self, spurning the very nature in which he was made. And he is a traitor to the Divine Governor of the universe, separating off his private individual soul from the community to which he belongs." And hence this lawlessness brings with it its appropriate recompense. "The sin committed punishes itself." "Each man's own fraud and foulness and iniquity beget the furies which torment him." Tiberius "found his evil deeds working in him their own chastisement. No acceptance in society, and no secession from it, saved him from himself. He owned to bosom torments and self-inflicted penalties." And even Nero, "approaching the temple of Vesta to worship, was suddenly seized with tremors, which sprang from the gods, or from the recollection of his crimes."

4. And hence the wail which has so often gone up from the sturdiest moralists, so similar to the final cry of the apostle, "*Who shall deliver me* from this inbred corruption which drags me down to death?" Look only at the mournful confession of Seneca: "What is this which while we are striving in one direction drags us along the opposite path? nay, while we are struggling to draw back from evil, drives us

into it? What is this, which is ever warring against our mind and hindering us from all steady determination? We are flung about like waves, tossed between opposite currents. We have no freedom of resolve, no thoroughness, no persistency. Do not tell me, It is simply human folly, always altering its wishes and its choice. For alas! how or when can we deliver ourselves from this folly? Who has power, of himself, to emerge from the whirlpool of its fluctuations? We need for this the hand of some one else. Some other than ourself must help us out." And listen to this cry, re-echoed from the far-off East, in the touching language of the Vedas: "I move along trembling, like a cloud driven by the wind; have mercy, Almighty! have mercy! Through want of strength I stray from the path; have mercy, Almighty! have mercy! Release me, like a calf from the rope that shackles it, that I may henceforth, set free from the service of sin, do service to my Lord!"

Thus the question of our book is the question

of human nature. It is no matter of narrow religious speculation, but of the universal moral life. It relates not to interpretation merely of Scripture, but to the interpretation of the holiest aspirations of the human soul. It responds to the cry not only of Paul and of the jailer, but of all humanity, "What must I do to be saved?"

And how have men endeavoured, of themselves, to answer this cry? What are the main solutions of the Problem of Redemption to which they have turned?

Plato thought to solve this problem by his elaborate scheme of social organization and State policy. And some likeness to this method reappears in the complications of modern secularistic Sociology.

The Stoics thought to solve this problem by stirring up in each individual that absolute moral power which they credited him with possessing. They called on the sovereign Reason to assert its supremacy, and then all rebels must fall beneath it. And an echo of this method we find among the Moralists of the last century, with their "Exert your energies," and their "Speak the commanding word 'I will,' and it is done!"

The Neo-Platonists, however, thought to solve this problem more by the force of contemplation than of resolve. They hoped to raise men above the perturbations of the senses through communion with the pure ideas of spirit.* This method has found a revival in modern Mysticism.

But apart from all the methods of Philosophy, Judaism had already thought to solve this problem of redemption from sin, by bringing in the influence of religious institutions, religious sanctions, and religious guardians. A sacred despotism was to hedge in every path of life with ceremonial observances, and direct every step of the humble disciple from the cradle to the grave. And this method is now being tried afresh by modern Sacerdotalism.

---

* "They rise above the region of obscuring mists, and sojourn in that which is their true fatherland, where they become partakers of true joy."—PLOTINUS.

Yet the failure of this method also has but too clearly manifested itself in both Jewish and Christian history. And more than this, the principle itself, of substituting outward submission for inward spontaneity, was long ago denounced by the Prophets of God; when they placed all their hope for the redemption of mankind in those "times of the Messiah," of which the one distinctive glory was to be the outpouring of God's Spirit upon all flesh; the transference of his law from tablets of stone to the fleshy tablets of the heart; and therewith the empowering of his people to be all righteous. This is the one divine scheme of Redemption which they looked for, to gather up and make successful whatsoever was true and good in all those other methods, of social organization, moral energy, intellectual contemplation, and ecclesiastical discipline. "I will *put my Spirit within you*, and *thus* will cause you to walk in my statutes, and keep my commandments and do them."

This, then, is the one solution of the problem

of redemption which has come to distinguish
"the last times," "the days of the Son of man;"
which has been brought out in all its clearness
by the coming of Christ; which constitutes
essentially the system of Christianity; and
which therefore Paul, as the Apostle of
Christianity, has set before us with such vivid
distinctness in this section of his Epistle. He
paints, therein, four consecutive phases of moral
experience, to which this redemptive process
brings the all-sufficient remedy. Glancing,
first, at the stage of *Security under sin*, in which
men naturally lie, the apostle shows next
how with our awakening to God's law and our
endeavour to fulfil it, there begins a deadly
Struggle against sin; which leaves us only
in helpless *Slavery to sin;* and ends with
that bitter *Suffering from sin* whence comes
the agonizing cry, Who is there to deliver
me? And then, while the evil, in all its progressive stages, is full before us, and our
personal sympathies with this picture are strung
to the utmost intensity, because we ourselves

are not ignorant of this evil in our own experience, he brings out the gracious Father, revealed in Christ, as supplying to every faithful combatant the *Hope* of Righteousness, the *Freedom* for righteousness, the *Life* for righteousness, and the *Power* for righteousness, through which alone he can change that first cry of despair, into the new outburst of gratitude, "Thank God, there is deliverance through Jesus Christ our Lord!"

CHAPTER II.

SECURITY UNDER SIN.

II.

WHEN Cudworth is writing about "the Christian's victory over sin," he says, "There are three general states of men in relation to God. First, of those who are alive to sin and dead to the law; whose consciences are not yet awakened to any sense of their duty, nor to the discrimination of good and evil; who sin freely, without check and without remorse. Secondly, of those who are alive at once to the law and sin; to the conviction of the one, and the power of the other; both these struggling within the bowels of the soul, and checking one another. This is a broken, confused, and shattered state, and such are, as Paul says, slain by the law. Third, of those who are dead both to the law and to sin, but alive unto God, the law of the Spirit freeing them from the law of sin. In the first state, which is the most deplorable of all, we are sin's freemen; *i.e.*, free to commit sin without check. In the second, we are God's bondsmen, serving God from fear, and under outward rules only. In the third, we are God's freemen, serving him in newness of spirit out of love to God."

Now it is the first state here mentioned on which we enter in this chapter; that state which, according to St. Paul's description of it, is one rather of *security under sin*. For since men in this condition have not yet become conscious of their relation to God's law, they are equally unconscious of any sin in their breaches of this law, and therefore are "alive," not to sin, but only to the ease and pleasure of unchecked enjoyment. For when the apostle says, "I was *alive* without the law at one time," he cannot mean, "I was exempt from all rule," since he is writing of himself as a representative Jew, from his very birth subjected to the law of Moses; but he means, "Though, under this law, I had no concern about my responsibility to it, no sense of its demands upon me, no experience of any effort to respond to those demands. The law was nothing to me. The sin of transgressing it was unfelt by me. I slumbered securely amidst golden dreams, with no hideous nightmare of responsibility sitting on my bosom, but with light-hearted self-complacency."

And this is a state of mind but too common with multitudes in every religious communion. How many there are who live on for years with little thought of the awful relation in which they stand to God; of the duties which from this relation spring; of the sin of indifference to these duties; of the account which they must one day give for such sin! Like Luther, who records his astonishment that "for seven long years he had been not only reading but expounding Holy Scripture so as to know it almost by heart, and yet had never discovered that whatsoever is not of God is necessarily of the devil." For always sensibility of conscience depends upon enlightenment of mind. Conscience is no blind instinct, but an acquired judgment emerging from comparing what we are with a standard that has dawned upon us of what we ought to be. "Young criminals," says one of our reports on prison discipline, "are found to have no greater pleasure than recounting to each other their various misdeeds and boasting of their cleverness." Just as St. Paul declares of the Gentiles that "they walked in the unfurnished emptiness of their mind, having the understanding darkened, being strangers to the life of God, through the ignorance that was in them, because of the blindness (want of moral insight) of their hearts;" so the first stage of the apostle's unconverted state was like the levity of childhood, with no apprehension of the *authority* of law, the *extent* of its demands, the *danger* of neglecting these demands.

1. Yet the *authority* of law St. Paul intimates by a single expressive word: "The law is *spiritual*." By which he means, springing from the divine Spirit, and backed, therefore, by the

divine sanction;* which thought he repeats in verses 22 and 25, where he calls it "the law of *God.*" A law, therefore, of no human invention; no imposition concerted by any number of men; no mere conventional set of rules made by society, by civil governors, by priestcraft, but sublime above these all. Recollect how emphatically this divine origin, with divine authority, was symbolized to the ancient Israelites. They had been rescued by the hand of Moses from Egyptian bondage. They had been led out by him triumphantly towards a new land, there to become established as a new nation. And he might well have taken upon himself to form a constitution for them. But no! Not on the ground of social prudence, not from the councils of collective wisdom, not as the dictatorial edict of a master mind, did Moses establish any law over those he had emancipated, but distinctly as the utterance of *God himself.* The hosts were assembled before

* See Theophylact: "Written by the Holy Spirit, through whose inspiration Moses enjoined it."

the sacred mount. A covenant was made with them by their divine Deliverer. He who had borne them as on eagles' wings, to make them his peculiar treasure, summoned them before him. And then, from the thick cloud, and the darkness, and the thunder and the flames of the inaccessible Sinai, from the awful seclusion of the divine throne, there came forth the new law for the new community :—" *The Lord* talked with them from the heavens, and *God* spake all the words of this law." And to secure the permanence of this authoritative code the same Voice afterwards summoned Moses to the royal presence, to put into his hands "tablets of stone," with this declaration, "These are the law and the commandments, which *I have written* that thou mayest teach them." Moses was not the author, but simply the mediator of eternal law. And its authority rested not on the temporary ruler of the nation, but on the unchangeable Sovereign of the world. "Why is the law called spiritual?" says Œcumenius. "Because it is the gift and, as it were, the public proclamation of the *Spirit of God.*"

Learn hence, that all true moral excellence is no mere product of a happy constitution, an inherited temperament, a favourable environment, a well-conducted education; but then first breathes its proper spirit when it is a *self-surrender to spiritual authority;* a study of "the good, and acceptable, and perfect will of *God;*" a filial imitation of the moral qualities of the moral Supreme; a labour to be holy as he is holy. Hence, in the Bible, we find not the self-sufficient term "virtue," but the humble phrase, "the fear of the Lord." "Behold, the fear of the Lord, that is wisdom, and the knowledge of the Holy One, that is understanding." "The fear of the Lord is a fountain of life to depart from the snares of death." And the law for every one of us has all the authority of the law from Sinai: "Ye shall do my injunctions and keep mine ordinances to walk therein, *for* I am *the Lord thy God!*"

2. But this law is called by the apostle

"spiritual" to intimate, not only the authority, but the *extent* of its demands. It is no superficial rule of parental guardianship, of family influence, of social restraints, of civil government; it penetrates into the deepest recesses and touches the most delicate vibrations of the *spirit* of man. We must say of it, as we say of its divine Author, "Whither can I go from thy Spirit, whither can I flee from thy presence? The darkness hideth not from thee; but the night shineth before thee as the day; the darkness and the light are both alike to thee!"

Thus, then, the divine Law applies, not, like the laws of men, to merely outward doings, but to the inward dispositions out of which doings spring. And hence the spiritual extent of all true morality. "What we are," says one, "springs out from what we think." "What you may not do in fact," says another, "that you must not begin to do in thought." "The law of justice," says Plato, "extends not only to external actions, but to the internal springs of action. For, once let a thought fill the mind, and we become captivated by it; and then desire goes on rising, like the three progressive notes of a chord, from the first to the third, and to the fifth." Whence Antoninus tells us, "My mother taught me to guard against, not only evil actions, but evil thoughts." And, "The highest and most sacred of all the works that God has entrusted to our responsibility is therefore the regulation of our thoughts."

Whence also comes the admonition of the Jewish sage, "Watch over thy heart above all other watchings, for out of it are the issues of life" (Prov. iv. 14-23). For "thorns and snares lie in the path of the untractable, and he alone who guards well his spirit can escape them" (xxii. 5). Whence, too, the warning of the Christian apostle, "Once let lust conceive, and its offspring will be sin; and sin when grown up to maturity, will bring forth death" (James i. 15). Hence the teaching of the Lord himself, "Fancy not that I am come to lessen the authority of Law; I am come to show you how much further it extends than the letter of the Mosaic statutes, even down into the thoughts and feelings of the heart. For the passion of anger is pregnant with murder; and the cravings of uncleanness are seedlings of adultery." And hence the Church, breathing the very spirit of her Master, explains, in her Catechism, the sixth commandment as forbidding all "malice and hatred in our heart;" and the seventh, as requiring us "to keep our body in temperance, soberness, and chastity;" and leads us, after each separate commandment, to pray for an inward spiritual obedience to it—"Incline our *hearts* to keep this law!"

Yet how many who listen to this prayer—nay, perhaps repeat it with their lips—are insensible to this *extent* of the obligations which it recognizes! Because they are not awake to their relation to him who seeth not as man seeth, but looketh on the heart. Everywhere there is spreading a godless Secularism; a living (that is) to the *age*, and not to the ages; a doubt of all reality beyond the present, the visible, the sensible; and a corresponding limitation of the tastes, the desires, the habits, the fears, and the hopes to the passing objects of a temporary existence. Hence men intrude the principle of Utility, which must always vary with varying circumstances, into the place of that Morality which is eternal as the heavens. Hence they assume a prudential conformity to the demands of social, civil, and national law to be all-sufficient for the regulation of our conduct. Or, worse still, oblige us for our self-direction not simply to apply the divine laws of propriety, but to work out by a sum in arithmetic the human chances of profit.* How different the axiom of Antoninus, that "we can never rightly discharge any duty to man if we shut our eyes to the close and inseparable connection of things human with things divine!" How contrary the teaching of our Master, "What is written in the Law? How readest thou? The first of all the commandments is, Thou shalt love the Lord thy God!"

* "Si le succés était le but de la vie, il n'y auroit pas de vertus, il n'existerait que des calculs."—MDME. DE STAEL.

3. But once more. To be "without the Law" is to be insensible, not only to its authority, and its extent, but also *to the danger of neglecting it.*

This danger follows from the very epithet with which the apostle characterizes the law of God,—it is "spiritual." For Œcumenius rightly notes as another meaning of this word, that the Law is called "spiritual" because "it not only springs from the Spirit of God, and extends to all the workings of the spirit of man, but, further, has in view, as depending on it, the *well being* of this spirit of man." The spirit of man is akin to the Spirit of God. It needs to be nourished by the Spirit of God. One means of such nourishment is the breathing into it of this Spirit by means of the Law of God. Without the knowledge, therefore, of this Law, the love of this Law, the feeding on this Law as manna from heaven, our spirit loses its proper sustenance; we can never grow up to our proper stature, we can never live our proper life. All things have their appropriate food, according to their kind. All things without this food must die. If we deny to the flesh its fitting nourishment, it withers and decays. And just similarly if we deny to the Spirit the food congenial to it, this too must wither and decay. There is no living without supplies of life. Moral starvation, therefore, must produce moral atrophy, and moral atrophy must end in moral death. We may be fully "alive" to other sorts of nourishment for other parts of our nature. We may cater zealously for the appetite of the flesh in all its various cravings for pleasure, pelf, and power; and we may find for a time, in such a diet, a zest, a luxury, a satisfaction like that of revellers at a feast; we may "nourish thereby our hearts as at a banquet, when our fatlings have been killed" (James v. 5). But meanwhile our real nature is defrauded of its necessary food; our very appetite for such food becomes weakened by neglect; we languish under spiritual atrophy; and so are dwindling down to spiritual death.

Yet the man of slumbering conscience has

no suspicion of this his perilous starvation. He has no notion that religion is as indispensable to his higher life as food is to his lower life. He regards it, if he can think of it at all, not as daily food, in order to his proper strength, and health, and joy, but only as an occasional cordial to be fled to in his moments of weariness of the world. Religion as (what its very name denotes) a binding *obligation* laid upon his very nature, involved in the very constitution of this nature; a necessity for the well-being of this nature; an indispensable means for raising him out of the flesh which clogs this nature into the proper action, life, enjoyment of the spirit which forms the essence of this nature, —such a thing has never entered into his dreams. He has never felt, like Job, "I have esteemed the words of God's mouth more than my necessary food;" nor cried with Jeremiah, "Thy words were found, and I did feed upon them, and they became to me the joy and the rejoicing of my heart!" And therefore the *danger* of neglecting this our proper, indispensable nourishment has never occurred to him. The sanctions of the Law have been to him only as outward threats, and not inward necessary consequences; and of such outward threats he has felt no more alarm than travellers in the higher Alps who behold the clouds spread out beneath them, and hear the mutterings of the thunder in the valleys in entire composure, for they have over them a clear serenity, unreached by all these lower perturbations. So the light-hearted worldling of easy-going morals and slumbering conscience imagines himself so lifted up above the common herd of low offenders as to be safe from all the danger which is rolling over their devoted heads. He fancies that by his education, his position in society, his standing in the Church, he is far above the region in which justly play the lightnings of divine wrath. "Why, then, mention hell to ears polite? The sky is clear above us. We have no great sins to startle us. We stand well with our family, our friends, our co-religionists. We have, indeed, perhaps, our failings. Who has not? But then, how merciful is God. He sent his Son, you know, to suffer in our stead. All, therefore, will, we trust, be well at last, *through Jesus Christ our Lord.*"

CHAPTER III.

STRUGGLE AGAINST SIN.

III.

WE have seen how the primitive condition of all men in relation to righteousness is one of Security under the absence of it. For where there is no sense of Law, or divine government, there is no sense of sin, which is disobedience to such government. And where there is no sense of sin, there is no fear about the consequences of sin: "I was at one time alive without the Law," following with childish levity my own will.

But this is only a temporary childhood, both of the race of men and of each individual man. There comes a time when some sense of government over us is aroused. For God's law is, like himself, "over all, blessed for ever." No one can entirely escape the range of its jurisdiction. The citizen of any earthly kingdom may fly beyond its confines and get naturalized under other, perhaps opposite, laws. But there are no confines to the kingdom of God. There is no spot in the universe not subject to his dominion. And therefore the first dawn of moral differences in us is also the dawn of a sense of responsibility. We open our eyes upon the splendour of the blazing, dazzling Law of God.

But with this also comes some admiration of this splendour; some feeling of its warmth and blessedness; some desire, therefore, to walk in the light of its divine radiance. Amidst all the corruption of our animal nature, the inward man is allured to righteousness, has been made in the image of righteousness, and therefore responds to righteousness as our proper end, our greatest good. A knowledge of righteousness awakens a will for righteousness.

And what results? The satisfaction of this will? The reduction of our whole being into harmony with it? Alas! nothing of the kind! For the apostle tells us that precisely along with the knowledge of Law, and the admiration of Law, and the will for Law, springs up from our lower nature a deep-set, inbred, obstinate antagonist to Law. "When the commandment became displayed to me, Sin started up therewith into active life!" The will for righteousness is met by a counter-will for unrighteousness. The struggle has begun between the law of our conscience and the law of sin. This struggle forms the subject of this chapter.

I. Look first at the new-born *will for righteousness*, which St. Paul commemorates.

Of such a will the apostle speaks again and again in the strongest terms. He assumes the awakening moralist to be not only made aware of his subjection to Law, but to recognise this Law as "holy and just and good;" the object of his necessary approbation, commending itself by its very apparition to his moral sense, and rousing in him a responsive will of fealty and obedience. "I know at once, from my inward responsiveness to its claims, that the

Law is spiritual, or pure and perfect in all its demands." "I consent to this Law that it is good." "I delight in this Law with my inward man."

Where the strength of the expressions is no proof of the Christian standing of the speaker. The note of Christianity does not lie in the vividness of the moral convictions, but in the vivacity of the spiritual life. All heathenism, naturalism, secularism, equally confess, "I discern, and do homage to, what is right though following what is wrong." And therefore we have, throughout this passage, no more than what both observation and experience tell us to be common to man. Notwithstanding some seeming exceptions among bold bad men, it is as "natural" for the human conscience, in proportion to its development, to admire righteousness, as to admire, under similar development, Truth and Beauty; the symmetry of Reason; and the harmony of sounds, of colours, and of forms. I remember but one seeming instance of the contrary, when Byron indulged his spleen against a lady who displeased him by calling her "ugly as virtue." But even here he was confounding virtue in the abstract with the specimen of virtue who disgusted him, for this same contemner of virtue is loud enough in his condemnation of those whom he thinks to have failed in virtue to himself; and thereby sets up virtue on her proper pedestal as the norm and pattern which others (at least) should reverence and imitate. Nor in all the manifold records and examples of human corruption can many be found who have not recognized a norm and law which the world, and even they themselves, ought to have obeyed. All self-reproach proves this. All outcries against the world prove this. The blackest pessimism proves this. For pessimism could never speak so ill of the universe if it had not before it some norm and law by which it thinks this universe *ought* to have been made and regulated. To detest darkness shows that we know and admire light. To denounce injustice, selfishness, sorrow, death, shows that we have some idea in us—nay, a hot love burning us—in relation to righteousness, benevolence, happiness, life. To cry out against evil is to assume that there is something essentially and intrinsically good!

And this intrinsic and essential goodness of the Law of God is what the sacred Lawgiver so beautifully symbolizes when he tells us that the elders of Israel saw beneath the Author of this Law "a paved work as of a sapphire stone, and as it were the body of heaven in its clearness." This Plato also extols when he says, " How manifold are those blessed types of beauty in the highest heavens on which it is given to the gods to fix their eyes! Nor are even we forbidden to behold this beauty in its clearness, when we at last begin to open our minds into symphony with the choir of heaven. Then, even we may hold high converse with the Supreme; we may become initiated into those sacred mysteries which delight the soul!" The leading Ideas of the divine Law;—the Ideas of personal self-possession and self-perfectionment; the Ideas of social regard for the rights, the deserts, and the wants of others; the Idea of religious self-subjection to him who has made these things the very joy of our nature as men; —these fundamental principles of all moral beauty "we come to delight in as the choir of heaven delights in them. They are to us as the stars that shine so calmly through the darkness of the sky. They are dearer to us than father and mother and brothers and sisters and closest friends. To them we give up all things else. For them we long with a desire never satisfied by night or by day. And our love for them is

> "'All made of faith and service;
> All adoration, humbleness, and duty;
> All purity, all loyalty, all observance!'"

Nor does the beneficence of God's Law, less than its beauty, win from the opening conscience the admiration, allegiance, will to serve, which are due to it. St. Paul tells us how he found this Law (and assumes therewith that all passing out of slumber into earnestness similarly find it) not only holy, just, and good, but having this additional recommendation to our observance of it, that it was "ordained to life"; *i.e.*, to open out to us the path and guide us in the way which issues in eternal blessedness. For what was the promise bound up with the first establishment of the Law among the Jews? "Ye shall do my judgments and keep mine ordinances; for if a man do this he shall *live by means of them*, saith the Lord" (Lev. xviii. 5). And what the reiteration of this point in the second publication of this Law? "The Lord commanded us to do all these statutes *for our good always*, that he might preserve us alive" (Deut. vi. 24). And what its confirmation by the authority of Jesus? "If thou desirest *to enter into life*, keep the commandments" (Matt. xix. 17). And how can this be otherwise from the very nature of this Law? For it is but the enactment by statute of the everlasting order which all things must conform to, both for their being and their well-being. All true blessedness comes ever, not as a purple ornament sewed on from without, but as the evolution of the pattern woven out from within; as the oil of gladness which plants of righteousness in their very growth distil; as the fragrance which by living and flourishing they exhale. "The fear of the Lord *tendeth* to life, and he that hath it shall therewith be satisfied."

And hence the necessary responsiveness to Law which springs up in every bosom in proportion as its beauty and beneficence unfold themselves to our moral vision. We cannot but answer to it, as the Hindoo hearers did to Bishop Heber, "Good! good!" We cannot but use the terms in which the apostle records his own experience, "I consent to the Law, that it is good." "I delight in the Law, in my inward man." For our moral taste goes over at once to the side of moral beauty, and looks lovingly upon it, as the model after which we have been fashioned, and by copying out which we may mould ourselves into the full proportions of humanity. Whence the immediate response of Israel to the Law propounded to them, "Behold the Lord our God hath showed us his glory and his greatness, and we have heard his voice; *we will hear it and do it.*"

II. Yet what comes next? Is it, what we might fondly have expected, the easy, happy accomplishment of this determination? the becoming in fact what we admire in theory? Alas! every one knows how just the contrary asserts itself! Every one knows how with the will for righteousness there is roused a *counter-will for unrighteousness.* Just when we purpose to do good we find present in us evil! Just in proportion as we find the pure and holy Law of God commending itself to our better nature, we find also a rebellion against this Law rising up in our lower nature; with which we must struggle without end. What says St. Paul? "When the commandment came to me" (disclosed in all its beauty and beneficence) "then, from that moment, Sin" (like a relentless slave-holder roused up to assert his despotism at the very first dawn of any desire for freedom in his bondsmen) "started into life and struck me dead" with disappointment and dismay. "Then did I discover residing in my members" (my animal nature) "a law antagonistic to the law awakened in my mind" (my rational nature), "and struggling to bring me down into captivity to the law of Sin!" Oh the unexpected apparition! Oh the malignant mockery with which it starts up before us! Just, then, when the sun of righteousness is shining on our conscience, the deep dark mist of inbred corruption forms itself into a terrible image of Unrighteousness! Has any one beheld in Alpine regions such a transformation?—the sun beaming on the mists of a ravine; the formation on them of a lovely rainbow; and lo! in the very midst of this radiance does there shape itself a vast dark spectre,—which is, in fact, the shadow of our own self! Just thus does the same light from heaven, which brings out before our well-pleased eye the rainbow splendours of God's Law, therewith project a shadow of *ourself* in hateful contrast with this Law; intruding into the very centre of this Law; so gigantically black and threatening that with terror we "become as dead."

Hence we learn the truth of Emerson's awful saying, "Our faith comes in moments, our vice is habitual!" Hence we join with Augustine in his humiliating confession, "What I marvelled at was, that when I really loved thee, my God, and no mere phantasm in thy place, I had no stability in this love. For when I was drawn to thee by thy beauty, too soon was I dragged back from thee by the weight of my own sinful habits, and became again, though with a groan, immersed in them. The *memory* of thee did indeed remain with me, nor did I lose my conviction about whom I should cleave to; but I doubted the possibility of my so cleaving, because my vitiated body enfeebled my mind, and my earthly habitation clogged my soaring thoughts. And thus, thrown back by intensified infirmity into my accustomed ways, there remained to me nothing but a memory of my love for thee, and a longing for sweets which I had scented but had no power to taste."

And thus commences our experience of a double nature; two wills in the same man; two souls in the same frame; the one waking up to God, the other waking up to thwart God; determined to suppress the rising rebellion in us against its ancient reign, and, like a strong man armed, to keep his goods in peace. Observe the strong expressions which St. Paul employs to characterise this new-born struggle with sin. "I should have had no experience of how the heart is set on lust" (literally a rushing onward over obstacles, a storming against Law*), "unless the Law had said to me, Thou shalt *not* lust. But when the commandment came before my consciousness, then sin, provoked by this interference with his reign, stirred up my latent propensity to evil into a raging passion for evil." Imagine a stream gliding calmly along, unnoticed, with no check, and therefore no responsive pressure against check; that is Paul's image of our nature in its unresisted

---

* Rom. vii. 7. For epithumia (lust) comes from thuo, to rush along, rage against.

tendencies. But then suppose some obstruction thrown across this stream, some barrier interposed to turn, or to retard, its course; at once what had been smooth begins to boil and foam; to beat against the dam, to surge above it, to sweep it altogether away. This is Paul's image of "lust," or natural propensity to sin, first thwarted, but soon stirred into a storm of passion, sweeping down the Law which would restrain it. Such is the *struggle with sin*, which comes from knowledge of Law, approval of Law, fidelity to Law,—a struggle to which political revolutions are as nothing, and yet which, like political revolutions, is the only method of emergence from a vitiated state into a new constitution and a new life. As indispensable as was the French revolution to the regeneration of France, as was the English revolution to the regeneration of England, so unavoidable is this moral struggle in the realm of our personality to the regeneration of our nature. There must come a "Holy War" in the City of Mansoul. All effectual medicines thus work.

Before they can cure they almost kill. The Law which was meant to bring us life, we find perverted to bring us death. Sin, laying hold of the commandment, intensifies the will of our lower nature against the will of God. When we are purposing to do the comely thing, there comes before us the spectre of an uncomely thing. "I saw," says Bunyan, "a parlour full of dust, because never swept; and when they began to sweep, the dust began so abundantly to fly about, that Christian was almost therewith choked. Now this dust is the original sin and inward corruptions that have defiled the whole of man. He who begins to sweep is the Law. And whereas thou sawest that, so soon as they began to sweep, the dust did so fly about that the room by them could not be cleansed, this is to show that the Law, instead of cleansing the heart (by its working) from sin, doth revive, put strength into, and increase it, in the soul; for *though it doth discover and forbid sin, it hath no power to subdue sin.*"

"Feeble at best is our endeavour;
 We see, but cannot reach, the height
 That lies for ever in the light;
 And yet, for ever and for ever,
 When seeming just within our grasp,
 We feel our feeble hands unclasp,
 And sink discouraged into night!"

CHAPTER IV.

SLAVERY TO SIN.

IV.

WE have seen how the first awakening of the mind to moral differences, while it brings with it some discernment of the beauty, the beneficence, and the authority of God's Law, brings with it at the same time a discovery of an inbred opposition to this Law, so aggressive and so powerful that St. Paul can do no less than impersonate it as a Demon in possession of us. And here begins a deadly struggle with sin.

Now there may be in struggle something noble, animating, bracing, elevating us above ourselves. War, it has been said, is the pioneer of civilization. It has its issues of good as well as evil; the man who is stirred up by it

> " Is happy as a lover, and attired
> With sudden brightness, like a man inspired,
> And through the heat of conflict keeps the law
> In calmness made."

And so it would prove with our moral warfare if our enemy were without us merely, and not within us. As Jesus towers up after his conflict with Satan, more godlike than before, with angels coming to do him service! "He became proficient in obedience by the things that he went through."

But, alas! such victory belongs only to the Son of God. How different the picture with the man depicted by St. Paul! With unassisted human nature the odds are utterly against us. The Adversary is too subtle as well as strong for us. He deludes us by means of our new-fledged aspirations. He trips us up by a back-stroke on our quivering limbs. And the conflict issues, not in triumph, but in tribulation. "We find a law in our members not merely warring against the law of our mind, but *making us captive* to the law of sin."

This is the result which the proudest moralists bewail when they confess that "we are made for something nobler than to be the slaves of our own lower nature, and tied and bound with a chain which eats into the soul"; that "any one who submits the divine within him to the tyranny of his ungodly nature is a hard-worked bondsman, and he alone who acts according to his better judgment can be esteemed a freeman"; for "no one is free who is in the service of bodily propensities."

Yet this is the condition of which our Lord reminds his hearers when they boasted of never having been in bondage to any one at any time. "What! never in bondage? when every one who does the work of sin is no other than the slave of sin!" This is the condition of which Paul warns the antinomian Romans: "Know ye not that to whomsoever ye yield up your allegiance, of him you make yourselves the slaves?" And this is what he pictures, in the paragraph on which we are now entering, as the state of every one, however awakened to the Law, who is not yet made alive in Christ.

1. Observe how *deep* is such a man's slavery to sin. He is hampered not by merely outward limitations; nor by human adversaries; nor by

those bonds of time and place and opportunity which make the strongest sensible of their weakness. No! the opposition is deep within his own nature. His own flesh is against him. His own propensities and cravings are mastering him. It is a home rebellion. "I discover a law *in my own members* warring against the law of my mind."

Here then we have disclosed to us that awful fact of "original, or birth sin" which our ninth and tenth articles declare to stand "not in the following of others, but in the fault and corruption of the *nature* of every one naturally engendered of the offspring of Adam; whereby we are *of our own nature* inclined to evil." Here we find that "wondrous thing" of which Pascal says, "Just the mystery in our nature which is most incomprehensible affords the only clue to the understanding of this nature. Our greatness on the one hand, our littleness on the other; our capacity for knowing God's will, and yet our incapacity for doing it; our admiration of his law, and yet our dislike of it; our wish to please him, yet our aversion to him; our purposes to obey him, and yet our treachery to these purposes—all these astonishing *facts* which one beholds in others and in ourselves, find their solution only as we recognize the deeper fact that in us, namely in our flesh, there dwelleth no good thing."

And note well how this recognition of "birth-sin," which the Rationalism of the last age branded with contempt as an Augustinian and Calvinistic slander upon human nature, is now substantiated, though on new grounds, by the favourite Philosophy of Facts. For according to this we are born, not, as men once fondly fancied, like sheets of pure white paper, to be written on by the hand of culture; but like palimpsests, scored and confused by cross superscriptions. We are survivals defiled by the deposits of ancestorial savages, animals, and mollusks. "Brain development, which is a matter of heredity, determines our character. On its quality and conformation depend our characteristics both intellectual and moral, our instincts of right and wrong. So that our mind is dependent on the physical growth of brain as the speed of a race horse is dependent on his muscular development."* Just therefore as the law of heredity clogs some with unshapely limbs and distorted features, with squinting eyes and deaf ears, this same law burdens others with disproportionate appetites, unruly propensities, misshapen affections, a squinting judgment, and a deaf conscience. We are not made by outward influences; we mar these influences by our inward malformation. We get not our character from our surroundings, but we impress on these surroundings our character. So true is the apostle's assertion that "in us, that is, in our flesh" (derived from our forefathers), "dwelleth no good thing."

2. "No good thing." For our inherited slavery to sin is as *wide* as it is deep. Mark the expression of St. Paul: "I find in myself, that is, in my animal nature, nothing whatever good." Because Sin, dwelling in this lower nature,

* *The Lancet.*

perverts to evil all the functions of our higher nature.

It perverts, for instance, our *perceptions* of God's law. In some clear night of contemplation, in some moment of secession from the glare of the world, the eternal principles of righteousness have shone so brightly over us that we have felt their magic influence drawing up our minds to high and heavenly things. Earth has become hidden from us. Its confusing noises have been hushed. Its artificial lamps have gone out. We are alone with the lights of heaven. We adore their steady brilliancy. We discern something of the beauteous order of their course. We follow them with wistful gaze in their majestic path. But how soon does intruding daylight dim, dissolve, disperse, this glorious vision! The earth wakes up again. Its murmurs distract our ear. Its scenes becloud our eye. The tumult of human opinions bewilders us. The customs of man draw off our attention from the laws of God. Falsehoods close to us put out truth far from us. And all that so lately drew us upward has vanished like a dream. "A deceived heart turns us aside, so that we cannot deliver our soul from the fumes of error, nor discern that we are grasping a lie in our right hand." So was it with the heathen of old. Light enough came forth from the things that were made to guide them to the Maker, yet their foolish heart was darkened. "Though they knew God's laws against sin, they nevertheless did this sin!"

But worse than this. Sin perverts also our *feelings* towards God's Law. Even when men have some perceptions of it, they become disloyal to it. They begin to ask, "Is it just and equal? Is it suited to our feeble limited nature? Is it better than a wandering meteor decoying us into a morass? Can it claim from us perfect fulfilment of all its superhuman demands? Must we not reduce our allegiance to it into some conformity with our powers, our position, our opportunities, the notions of our circle, the habits of our age, the requirements (in short) of 'common sense'? Is the Law more than an Ideal, never to be realized by feeble man? All very well for divines to enlarge on its unsullied purity, but what comes of such exaggerations? You make only enthusiasts or hypocrites. You delude the simple into aspirations, efforts, struggles, after an over-much righteousness which destroys them, while you encourage the cunning to put on the mantle of philosophy or the cloke of religion for selfish ends." "One shrinks," says Madame de Sévigné, "from giving oneself up to God, because his Law seems hard, and one does not like to destroy oneself. If we seek to pay all our debts to it, we shall ruin ourselves."* Well enough for some, to read romance, and indulge in the dreams of an aspiring spirit, excogitating from the depths of their deluded consciousness Platonic republics, Utopian societies, millennial purities, the return of Astræa, the reign of righteousness; but—come down into world, where all of us must get our living, condescend to its necessary occupations,

* "On se ruine quand on veut s'acquitter."

its indispensable compliances, its unavoidable defilements, its one great reigning principle of *compromise* in everything, and tell me if the airy visions of ecstatic lawgivers, prophets, and apostles can ever be condensed into solid substance; if men can live like angels; if poetry can become prose; if romance can be reduced into reality in this unquixotic world? Has, in fact, the law of Moses, after all the enforcements of Scribes and Pharisees, ever been fulfilled? Have the splendid visions of Ezekiel ever become realized? Are the glories of the Apocalypse more than heavenly types? Must not the whole world be swept clean of its buyers, and sellers, and money changers, before it can become the Temple of God's holiness?

> " Whither is fled the visionary gleam?
> Where is it now, the glory and the dream?"

And what follows, too often, from such disloyal feelings towards God's law, but a recalcitrant *will* against this law? Men pass from regarding the demands of righteousness as shadowy and unreal, to regarding them as delusive, nay, a mockery. They adopt the tone of persons played with, deceived, like children by a bugbear. And this brings with it repulsion, resistance, a determination to pull off the gigantic mask which would scare them into submission. Thus it was that the tempter seduced into rebellion Adam and Eve. "What! can you possibly believe that God has planted in your garden a tree of wisdom and then with churlish jealousy forbidden you to profit by it? You cannot think he intends to keep you in perpetual childhood, instead of training you up into your rightful manhood? Or, will you tamely submit to such despotism? Will you not claim the privilege of your birthright as made ideally in the likeness of God, and therefore to be educated up to actual conformity with God?" And thus it was not to the gratification of some capricious appetite subversive of God's Law, to which the devil tempted them, but to the questioning, intellectually, the justice of this Law.

And this suspicion of God and of his dealings with us has continued ever since. Look at the Israelites. Honoured above all nations with direct communications from on high, how did they regard the sacred gift? The terror which seized them when they "stood afar off" from the holy mount; the eagerness with which they entreated Moses, "Speak thou with us, and we will listen, but let not God speak with us, lest we die;" betray a secret repugnance to the divine interference. They rejoiced in the first announcement concerning their *privilege*, "Ye shall be to me a peculiar treasure," and responded to it readily, "All that the Lord hath spoken we assent to." But when the awful Voice proceeds to enunciate their corresponding *duty;* and *law*, with its restrictive regulations, throws its thundering "Thou shalt not" on their free action and free will; then, the inborn rebelliousness of flesh to spirit, of the animal body to the regulating mind, of the individual will to the Supreme will, breaks out, and hoping to be able to cope with Moses, the man, stands off with aversion from Jehovah, the unbearable God.

And is not this a fault and corruption of the nature of every one? Does not sad experience tell you that "the heart of man is not only deceitful above all things, but *wilfully contumacious?*"* Tell a child not to pass a certain boundary; it becomes curious, tentative, restless, unsatisfied till it has made the forbidden stride. Find in yourself some high call summoning you to duty; does not the very sound awaken the most revolting contradictories? "When the spiritual personality is at its highest, then come evil suggestions in the form of an unspiritual, diabolical personality."† When Jesus was most full of the Spirit, and most absorbed in meditation on the best way of accomplishing the work assigned to him as the Son of God, then comes the tempter with

---

* Jeremiah xvii. 9. Where the Chaldee version uses the same word that is rendered in Daniel ii. 40, "*strong as iron.*"

† Coleridge.

his plausible suggestions of wrong ways of procedure. Nay, our very prayers against sin often stir up sin. The self-mortifications of a St. Anthony rouse the seductive forms he seeks to keep down. Into the very sanctuary of the spirit there comes the stubborn protest of the everlasting No! At the very moment, and because of the very fact, of your drawing around you the magic circle of sanctity, there crowd about this circle the hideous shapes of unclean spirits, mocking, tempting, threatening, stretching over to catch the slightest indication of a blanching cheek, an unsteady eye, a wavering will, that they may leap the excluding barrier and break the charm.

"To what man's spirit conceives
Of purest, best, some demon form still cleaves;
High feelings that in us to life give birth,
Are numbed, and wither in the poisonous breath of earth."

CHAPTER V.

SUFFERING FROM SIN.

V.

THE young and inexperienced are continually being duped into the gross mistake that happiness consists in folly and self-will; nay, that the *zest* of pleasure lies in its unlawfulness: "Stolen waters are the sweetest, and bread devoured in secret thence derives its savour." And hence the word "life," so expressive of all that is healthy in our nature, comes to denote the morbid agitations of this nature. To "live while we live" is to "seize the pleasures of the passing day." And the very men who by their excesses are murdering life are called, by an undesigned irony, in pre-eminence "Livers of life" (Viveurs).

Yet nothing is more certain, and nothing more certified by such men's own experience and confessions, than the terrible fact that a life of lawless pleasure becomes a life of pain; that self-indulgence is self-destruction; that the slave of sin soon feels the cruel stripes of slavery; that "whosoever hath a froward heart findeth no good" (Prov. xvii. 20); and that though men may "kindle a fire and cheer themselves with brilliant sparks, and walk exultingly in the light of their fire and in the sparks that they have kindled, the end must be that they lie down in sorrow" (Isaiah l. 11). We have not Scripture proof alone for this; we have the concurrent testimony of all observers of the course of things. "Never does avenging Jove entirely lose sight of the man who has broken his laws. One transgressor, it is true, he may punish sooner than another; yet at last the fatal consequence must come to all." Nay, "this fatal consequence is already coming, though with stealthy step, along with the lawless pleasure itself." "No bad man, therefore, can be happy." "As surely as righteousness tendeth to life, so surely whosoever pursueth evil pursueth it to his death."

This is what St. Paul insists on in the passage

under our consideration. The body he calls "a body of *death*," because from out of the misuse of our lower nature by sin grows up the punishment of this misuse. Not the accidents of outward circumstance, not the stripes of judicial vengeance, not the flames of a local Gehenna; but the worm that gnaws and the fire that burns the inward conscience,—these constitute our "death." Out of dis-order springs dis-ease Our suffering under sin becomes that of the bondsman, conscious of his bondage, hating his bondage, struggling against his bondage, and yet finding no relief but in that final exclamation of despair, "O wretched one* that I am! who is there that can free me from this body of death!"

1. This is the cry, first, of conscious *self-contradiction*. It is the suffering that springs from

---

* This is a word expressive of the deepest misery; a favourite with the Greek tragedians for unspeakable woe; and used by Epictetus to denote self-loathing as well as self-commiseration. "What am I? A wretched diminutive sample of humanity in a miserable bit of flesh!"

the experience the Apostle had been before confessing, "What I do I disapprove of, what I hate that do I!" Nay, "even when I most earnestly resolve to be good, I find no means of realizing what seems so fair to me!" For such a state of moral experience *must be* one of suffering. As often, and as intensely, as we feel it, it must destroy our happiness. For happiness is, according to the emphatic Hebrew term for it, "Peace;" that is, the harmony of thought and feeling and will and action; the balance of all our powers in perfect self-adjustment, the correspondence of our doings with our determinations; our conduct with our convictions; "the symphony" (as Clement puts it) "of all the chords of our being." Yet just this "peace" is what the baffled wrestler for righteousness cannot obtain. There is no music in his soul. His ear is tortured by the discords of unmodulated passion. "His noble and most sovereign reason is like sweet bells jangled, out of tune, and harsh!"

You find this where you would least expect

it. The Stoics are usually censured as a self-sufficient sect. In theory they may be so. They paint their "wise man" as "that faultless monster whom the world ne'er saw." Whence St. Simon calls the Stoic "a fine and noble chimæra." "How easy is it" (they maintained) "to drive out every disturbing thought from the mind, and reduce it to a perfect tranquillity!" "For the sovereign reason is the sole cause of its own discomfiture. You would succumb to no disorder of soul, *if* you did not your own self yield obedience to the seditious movements of the fancy. You are secure from all subserviency *if* you will not make yourself subservient."* But, alas! "there is much virtue in an *if*," and this "if" vitiates their whole system. For when you turn to fact, nay, to the personal confessions of the noblest Stoics, you find this tall talk is *ideal* only. It is like Bishop Butler's beautiful picture of the supremacy of *conscience*, which some take as if true of *the* conscientious *man*, but which turns out to be only a sovereignty

* See Antoninus, v. 2, vi. 16.

de jure of right divine, but not *de facto* in the actual struggles of life. Whence comes, to all these most exalted theorists, the bitter suffering of *self-contradiction*. "Remember," says the Emperor, not yet imperial over self, "how long you have *put off* your attainment of inward serenity. For shame! for shame! How long will you go on to affront and dishonour your own self! how long will you *suffer your reason to be enslaved* and made the puppet of rebellious passions!" And Seneca confesses, "We need some help in this our warfare, till the knot be untied and all our mortal chains be broken. For, alas! the most successful has only slightly loosened these chains! He is not yet free, but only on the road to freedom. I have not yet reached to spiritual health, I never shall. I am only using palliatives for my disorder. I have not yet won the race, I am only running the course. All our wisest men have taught, not what they themselves are living up to, but what *ought* to be their life. Not therefore what I actually do, but what my conscience tells me *should be* done, this is what I gaze at with admiration, this the goal towards which, at a long, long distance, I am creeping on."

And who does not groan, with moral misery, under such self-contradiction? We discover it then most clearly when we are most in earnest. Darkness is discerned only by means of light; the strength of a current when we begin to stem it; the swiftness of a locomotive only through the crash of opposition to it. And the more men have sought, by their own strength alone, to thwart, to starve, to torture the rebellious nature, the more have they been startled at its power :—

> " All their fences, and their whole array,
> One cunning bosom-sin blows quite away."

2. And hence comes, next, the wail of *self-despair*. "Who is there that can free me from this body of death?" A final confession, after all his struggles, that never can he free himself. The very term by which he designates himself ("O wretched one") is used of the hopeless

labour of a convict in the mines. All the bright visions of the moralist have been clouded over with black night. All the zeal of the Pharisaic legalist has only proved the law to be a yoke that no man can bear. "My insight into what is right cannot deliver me. My love of what is right cannot deliver me. My struggles for what is right cannot deliver me. And the very Law which I adore as holy, just, and good, cannot enforce its precepts on me against the antagonistic wickedness of my own flesh. And who then can deliver me from this wickedness? Who?"

Whence mark what is included in this "who." It is just like the cry of the Psalmist groaning under Babylonian slavery, "*Who* will give the salvation of Israel?" It is the yearning for a *Person* of sufficient power to confront the *personality* of the tyrant king; a *Will* that can conquer all opposing wills. It is like Elymas the Sorcerer, when he felt his blindness, "going about seeking *some one* to lead him by the hand." The cry of the exhausted moralist is not for *things,*—abstractions, notions, some new principle of action, some new system of discipline, some new and stronger moral reasonings, philosophic speculations, theological dogmas. No! For it has been truly said, "When you get me a good man made out of arguments, I will get you a good dinner by reading you the cookery book." What was enslaving Paul was a *power;* and a *power* therefore he must get to break his chains. The sick man can make nothing of a treatise on physic,—he calls for a physician. The oppressed man will never get his rights out of a digest of law,—he sends for a lawyer. The bankrupt will gain nothing from a dissertation on bankruptcy,—he must find a surety to discharge his debts. The theory at the head of the American declaration of right, that "all men are by nature free," was of no use to the slave in the Southern States till *men* arose with a will, a tongue, an arm, and a sword to make him free. The Israelites would have languished for ever in Egyptian bondage had not their "sighing and crying" to a divine *Power* brought from this *Power* a human *Person* to break their chains. "They sighed by reason of their bondage, and they cried; and their cry went up to *God*, by reason of their bondage; and *God* looked upon the children of Israel, and *God* said to Moses, I have seen the oppression wherewith the Egyptians oppress them; come now, therefore, and I will *send thee* to bring forth my people out of Egypt."

And, just similarly, nothing short of this, a personal interposition, is the method by which alone the last despairing cry of men groaning under sin can be responded to. "When we were yet *without strength* in ourselves, *Christ* came, to die for the ungodly." "When we were in bondage under the Law, *God sent his Son*, made under the Law for the very purpose of delivering those under the Law, that they might receive *the adoption of sons.*"

CHAPTER VI.

HOPE OF RIGHTEOUSNESS.

VI.

IT is part of the skill of a great artist to heighten the vividness of his pictures by broad contrasts of colour and light and shade. Who knows not Rembrandt's excellence in this?

Now Paul is the Rembrandt of moral painting. He is fond of contrasts strongly brought out, highly coloured, with bold lights and shadows. Look at 1 Cor. vi. 9-11, "Fornicators, adulterers, idolaters, such were some of you;"—how black the tints of what they had been; "but now ye are washed, made sacred, set all right with God;"—how bright the tints of what they are! Look again at his letter to the Romans;—the awful darkness of his picture of the unconverted Jews as well as heathen in chap. i. 24-32, ii. 17-24, contrasted with the glowing light of his picture of the new-born

Christian in chap. v. 1-5. Look further at the still more finished portrait of the passage from Death to Life, which we are studying in this book. It is drawn from himself; it is ideally true for all men; yet the shadows are laid on so deep on the one side, and the lights coloured up so high on the other, that looking on this picture and on that we cry, "Hyperion to a Satyr!" The portrait in chapter vii. is inscribed in black letters, "Wretched man that I am!" but that which follows, in golden characters, "Thank God through Jesus Christ our Lord!"

Now to understand this second portrait we must keep before us the first. For the contrast was *begun* by this great painter in chap. vii. 5, 6: "When we were living only in the flesh (as men of this present evil world), sin wrought in us to our death; but now that through participation in Christ's death and resurrection we are living in a world of spirit, we serve God, henceforth, with a new obedience." And after the long digression, in chap. vii. 7-25, to vindicate the Law, this contrast is restated in chap. viii. 1-3 in the very same terms as before. The apostle declares himself and his fellow-Christians to have been brought out from the region of Law and its concurrent sin and destruction, into that new region of Spirit, wherein there is supplied to them, through Christ's teaching and work, the Hope of Righteousness, the Freedom for Righteousness, the Life for Righteousness, and the Faith for Righteousness, from which alone springs the power of new obedience, and its resulting bliss.

Let us see in this chapter how there comes to us the *Hope of Righteousness.*

It is a certain fact that practical action depends on theoretical conception. What we do is regulated by what we feel, and what we feel depends on what we think. It is according to our hopes or fears, our belief of bondage or liberty, our outlook towards the possibilities of things, that we become weak or strong in the work of life. Our ability varies as our sense of ability. And hence, no courage without confidence; no power without presumption of power; no strength, therefore, for righteousness without some hope of righteousness. The greatest temptation to "recklessness of unclean living" is always "I cannot help it! It is no use. What good of trying, when I have never yet succeeded, and I never shall!" Whence the first step of recovery in morals, as in every other effort of will, depends upon encouragement to try. You see this even in animals. Who has not observed the tired beast of burden, when kindly soothed, spoken to, handled with the slightest help, burst into a new spring and make its way? And so with the burdened labourer after righteousness. Encouragement is his first necessity. A hopeful word, a sympathising look, the slightest testimony from another's experience,—above all, some putting forth of another's hand, awake new expectation, and therewith new effort.

Now just such Hope of Righteousness is roused for the wrestling moralist in that new region which is opened out to him in Christ. Mark well the striking contrast beginning in chap. vii. 25, with all that had gone before, from vii. 7. The last cry in the old state of things had been "O me miserable!" the first in the new state of things is "Thanks be to God!" The last feeling then, as to the sinner's outlook, was, "Who shall deliver me from death?" *i.e.*, condemnation; the first feeling now is, "*no* condemnation!" And all this thorough change because of that single fact noted in viii. 2, that the one mark of the new dispensation in Christ is "Spirit," as opposed to the one mark of the old dispensation of Moses, which was "Law." Throughout the former passage reigns nothing but Law. For even though God in some portions of his previous revelation had given such gracious intimations of love, these had come to be obscured by the perpetual interferences of Law; Law, as a rigorous, relentless, arbitrary code of social, political, ritual, and ecclesiastical *literal* prohibitions and literal prescriptions, most appropriately written on tablets of *stone*. In all the apostle's picture of the legalist striving against sin, there is no reference to *God*, as a Person, a sympathising Friend, a Helper to whom he might look up in his endeavours after righteousness. The whole contest is carried on by the labouring will of the moral athlete, between the cold light of the Law looking down upon him from its inaccessible height, and the feverish impulses of sin close to him in his flesh. And that hard, imperious Law has not a word of encouragement for him, not a grain of sympathy, not an atom of help, not even the power to enforce its own authority,—nothing but an awful threat of judgment and fiery vengeance on his failure. For President Garfield has truly said, "Coercion is the basis of all law. A law is no law without coercion." And Moses has said, "Cursed is every one that continueth not in all things that are written in the book of the Law, to do them!"

But turn to the contrasted picture by St. Paul, and you come out at once from the realm of relentless Law into the realm of relenting love.

Precisely at the point where the form of sin as your antagonist has widened and darkened into its most terrifying blackness, as the shadow of Death, there is revealed as your protector the form of God, in Christ, in radiant light. By a hideous personality you have been driven to desperation; by a gracious personality you are roused to hope. The whole stress of that new exclamation is laid on this word "*God.*" "Who is there to deliver me?" "Behold, in Christ, *the God* who will deliver you!" Just as in the parallel passage, 1 Cor. xv. 56, 57: "The sting of death is sin, and the strength of sin is the law; but *thanks be to God* who giveth us the victory through our Lord Jesus Christ!" "*God* was in Christ, reconciling the world to himself."

It is important to dwell upon this contrast, because all religion, from its lowest to its highest forms, is no mere belief of abstract principles, but is a living trust in some living person who can bring us practical help. It is the flying in our weakness to some *Power* believed to be stronger than our enemies and ourselves. The birth of individuality lies in the discovery of other individualities by whom we are influenced, on whom we depend. But these individualities we soon find to be themselves under influence, themselves dependent upon forces beyond our ken. To such forces, therefore, the feeble make appeal, they try to win them over to their side by offerings such as they are wont to find acceptable to their fellow-men. And hence the worship of the Fetisch, or symbol of unseen power, as a refuge from all known limitations.

But then, these unseen powers are often found to fail their worshippers. They seem to be themselves unable to do all we ask of them; they are clearly, therefore, themselves limited by higher powers, dependent upon stronger masters. Hence the next step in religion, from the hidden forces of earth into a region transcending earth. Men raise their eyes to the sun, the moon, the stars, as showing their lordship over earth by regulating seasons, and days, and years. The worship of the heavenly bodies is the second stage of ascent from weakness to strength.

Yet even these heavenly bodies exhibit change. They appear and disappear. They are dependent, in both the rate and the direction of their course, on somewhat higher than themselves; the vast expanse in which they move must be superior to all that in it moves. Hence a higher court of appeal is opened to us. "Heaven" becomes the name for a Power dominant over the host of heaven. To this, therefore, we transfer our worship. Its blue serenity we accept as its favouring smile; its black tempests as its withering frown.

Nor do we stop there; these very changes in the aspect of heaven suggest to us instability, dependence, subjection. Above the highest heaven, therefore, there must be enthroned a higher than the heavens, one who can make them at one moment propitious, at another destructive, to us. The pure serene must be the lifting up of *his* countenance on us; the thunder the growl of *his* displeasure; the lightning the arrows of *his* vengeance. Whence comes that fourth stage of religion, to which such magnificent utterance has been given by the poets of old?—" In the beginning *God* made the *heavens* as well as the earth;" " I, even my hands have stretched out the heavens, and all their hosts have I commanded;" " I clothe the heavens with blackness, I make sackcloth to be their covering;" "*The Lord* is my guardian, the Lord my shade upon my right hand. The sun shall not shine on me by day, nor the moon by night, for *the Lord* shall preserve me from all evil."

But, next, we need a refuge, not merely from physical evils, from earthly enemies, from the malign influence of nature's forces, but from inward foes more dangerous than they all. For we are essentially *moral* beings, and have to wage a moral warfare, and fall through weakness into moral defeat and shame and self-reproach, and yearn for a moral helper. And where shall we look for this but in him whom we already recognise as supreme in nature and events? Nay, how should we not necessarily look for this in him, who has given us this our moral nature; who is himself the Ideal of this moral nature; who therefore must love righteousness above all our love of it, and hate iniquity above all our hatred of it; and who consequently must be ready to help us in our efforts to be righteous? Will the accomplished artist, or sage, or proficient in any excellence, be prodigal of sympathy and of support to all who are enamoured of this excellence; and will not the First Fair and Wise and Good stretch out a gracious hand to every one who is toiling to be like himself? It has been well said, "By desiring what is perfectly good, even when we cannot do it, we make ourselves part of the divine power against evil, widening the skirts of light and rendering the struggle with darkness narrower,"* and will not he who is light, and in whom there is no darkness, make himself part with us in this endeavour? "Try then" (says Antoninus) "if God will not help you in this work. Put him to the test by prayer, and see

* " Middlemarch," iv., 308.

what will come of it. Assuredly, if God works along at all with men, he will especially work along with you for moral ends. Pray, therefore, that you may be relieved by him from fear of outward things, from hankering after outward things, from grieving over their presence or their absence; pray that you may desire nothing evil, and be averse to nothing that he appoints, and then, I say again, see what will come of it!"

For the sure trust that such prayer will bring the help we need pervades every godly soul. The Egyptian wise men declare, "The righteous is at one with God. He communes with them and they with him, and the light of his countenance shines upon them." The Vedas say, "He who dwelleth in thine innermost nature, the God of righteousness, is for ever near thee." Zoroaster assures us, "Though truth is combated by falsehood, and righteousness by unrighteousness, not for ever will this war be carried on. For all that truly *is* triumphs over what is not; and righteousness therefore must gain the day. Ormuzd reigns supreme to Ahriman over all the incidents of existence; and enables all into whom he breathes his life to fight out their battle with evil till they conquer." Confucius maintains that "the heavens are righteous, rewarding good and punishing evil." Plato teaches that "virtue comes neither from inward nature nor outward discipline, but solely from God." Seneca affirms that "then only will the way of life become easy for us when we tread it with prayer, and by the side of God. For he who has made us for righteousness does most assuredly give his help to every labourer after righteousness." And Cleanthes therefore prays, "O thou Giver of all good gifts, save thou poor man from his baneful inexperience, and grant to him that wisdom, by means of which thou art thyself the righteous Governor of the universe!"

And we need not be reminded how to this same trust in God as making for righteousness the Bible invites us in every page. From the friendship of the Lord vouchsafed to Abel, to Enoch, to Noah, to Abraham, on to the ample promises of his prophets, and thence to the final manifestation of himself in Christ, he has proclaimed himself the helper of all who love his law. "The King's strength loveth justice. Thou dost establish equity, thou dost set up justice and righteousness." "I the Lord love righteousness. I will reward them who labour after it. I will make with them an everlasting covenant." And our divine Master therefore sets out in the very front of the demands he is going to make for strict obedience to God's Law, this encouragement, "Cheer up, all ye who are hungering and thirsting after righteousness, for ye shall certainly, some time or other, be filled therewith;" nay, passes on from inspiring hope to confirming this by promise: "If ye cannot refuse your children that which is essential to their bodily sustenance, how much more may you be certain that your Heavenly Father will vouchsafe to you that Holy Spirit which gives life and sustenance to the soul!" "Ask, therefore, and ye shall have ; seek, and ye shall find ; knock, and it shall be opened to you!" "The things which are impossible by human power alone, these become possible with God upon your side!"

CHAPTER VII.

FREEDOM FOR RIGHTEOUSNESS.

VII.

WE have seen how in Paul's picture of the process of recovery from sin to salvation, he paints the convert first as lying in a state of insensibility to sin; next, as waking up into a state of conflict with sin; and finally, as landed in a state of triumph over sin. In the first stage the animal life is predominant. In the second, the intellectual life; not till the third is there begotten that spiritual life which works out righteousness.

And this spiritual life is derived entirely from Christ; from our participation in his death, his resurrection, his spirit, and our thus being made citizens of that higher world in which he lives and reigns.

The first object brought before us in this new sphere is God the Father interested in our righteousness; God in Christ bringing back the world unto himself, and therefore holding out the hope of righteousness even for such helpless sinners as ourselves.

The second is the more specific presentment of this Heavenly Father as having prepared the way for this righteousness, and making it possible for us to set out in pursuit of it, by *freeing us from all the penalties of sin*, which in our hopeless struggle we have incurred. We have seen already how the feeble wrestler with inbred corruption groans under the terror of that ruin which he sees before him, yet knows not how to escape from. Especially how this wrestler, as a conscientious *Jew*, with all the shackles of his iron Law encumbering him and weighing him down, found this Law, though intended for his good, turned into an occasion for exasperating the sin which was destroying him. The Law, while strong in authority, was found by him weak in influence. Its demands for righteousness were overborne by the corruption which it sought to root out. "A law in our members resisted the law in our mind, and made us captive to the law of sin." And then, with broken Law comes a broken heart. With duties unfulfilled comes dread acuminated. For this Law has its penalties as well as its precepts; the breach of it, therefore, rouses in us a sense of *guilt* as well as of sin, of danger as well as of disappointment; the transgressor finds that even if he had the power to satisfy the Law in time to come, he has nothing wherewith to satisfy the Law for the time past. He is like a debtor who, the more he struggles to meet his liabilities by bill drawn after bill, and renewal after renewal, has only thereby made his ruin more inevitable. "How can I pay my way in the future, with these claims unsatisfied in the past? What remains for me but to lie down and die?" I once saw a city acquaintance standing on the kerb-stone of the Royal Exchange, gazing out into vacancy, with no eye for myself or the busy throng around him, with a countenance so blank, so corpse-like, that it still haunts me at a distance of sixty years;—and the first news I heard on the morning following was his self-inflicted death! *There* was a picture of the defaulting steward: "My lord is hard! He will sell me up, with all that I have! He will give me to the torture till my payments be made!"

Now what is the one sole method by which this deadly despair may be removed? It is that announced long ago by the Prophet Isaiah when he drew away the heart of his people from their useless sacrifices to direct communion with God: "Cease to do evil, learn to do well; then come and we will settle our differences, saith the Lord! Though your sins be as scarlet, they shall be white as snow; though they be red like crimson, they shall be as wool; only be willing and obedient, and ye shall eat the good of the land!" It is that enforced with still more vividness by our Lord in his two parables about the insolvent servant. When the man was loaded with debt; when he could do nothing but simply fall down prostrate with the earnest supplication, Lord, have patience with me! "then," says Jesus, "his master was moved with compassion towards him, and *loosed him from his bonds*, and forgave him the debt;" or, as St. Luke adds, "frankly," without any conditions more, forgave him "*all* that debt." And just this, therefore, is what St. Paul has painted as God's method with the despairing sinner. As in our Lord's parable there was nothing left for the debtor but simply to cry out in prostrate supplication, " Have patience with me!" and then came the immediate answer of compassion, "Loose him from his bonds;" so in the picture by St. Paul, directly on the cry "Who shall deliver me!" comes the exclamation "Thank God," for he has delivered us! he has freed us in Christ from all our liabilities in the past, that we may set out with unshackled liberty to serve him better for the time to come!

And how does St. Paul give vividness to this blessed assurance? Remember, he was a Jew writing to Jews. He and they had constantly before them the solemnities of the old sacrificial

Law. He and they were familiar from their infancy with the direction in this Law, "If any one doeth somewhat against any of the commandments of the Lord, and be *guilty*, let him bring his *offering* for his sin which he hath sinned, and the priest shall burn it on the altar for a sweet savour to the Lord, and the priest shall make an at-one-ment" (a setting him *at one* with God,*) "for his sin that he hath committed; *and it shall be forgiven him.*" And therefore, in the terms of this sacrificial Law, according to the symbolism of this sacrificial Law, Paul now describes the freedom to which God in Christ raises up every penitent, and the complete immunity which he vouchsafes from all the penalties due to sin. "Just as, in old time, the sacrificial offerings of our Law released us from the curses of this Law, just so, now, God, sending his Son in a body like that which is in us the seat of sin, to bear in our stead the guilt of sin, has inflicted on this body of his Son the

---

* "I will do my benevolence to make *at-one-ments* and *compromises* between you."—SHAKESPEARE.

penalty of sin, that we may be freed therefrom. Look on his sufferings as your sufferings, his death as your death, that so his life may become your life, his righteousness your righteousness, his rewards your rewards!"

Now how shall we get the full force of this comparison so vivid for Jews, and make the freedom it proclaims our own? Only by seizing the pure *Idea* thus symbolized to us. Always, on every subject, to profit by the forms conveyed to us in words, we must penetrate through these forms to the *Ideas* imbedded in these words. The modes of expression, all alive to older times and people, but now dead to us, must be replaced by such as we can enter into History must be turned into experience. "It is not so much" (says Ferrier) "by reading Plato as by studying our own minds in the light which Plato has contributed, that we can *find out* what his ideas are. It is only by verifying in our own consciousness the discoveries of others that we can understand them." * As another writer

* Ferrier, Lectures, i., 328.

says, "Before, I only knew it; now, I have *found it out.*" For only by living through a thing do we find it out. No one knows a headache but by feeling it. No one, the glow of admiration but by admiring. No one, the expansiveness of love but by loving. Who can convey any notion of benevolence to the selfish? Who of gratitude, to the cold-hearted? Who of friendship, except to the sympathetic? Who of faith, except to the trustful? Who of prayer, except to the needy?

And just so fares it with the apostolic idea of Christ dying for our sins. We must realize the feelings of the Jew of old. We must see him overwhelmed with his sense of guilt as a transgressor of the Law; and seeking the relief this Law prescribes. He brings his sacrifice. He has it slain for him before the altar. He gazes as the blood of it is sprinkled before the Lord. He watches the incense of it steaming up as a sweet savour to the Lord. And so the burden falls off from his trembling soul; the penalty dreaded by him has been turned on to another head; and he "goes down to his house justified,"—*i.e.*, standing right with the Supreme—to begin now, with a new heart and new hope, a new life. Just so, Christ's death is to guarantee to us a recovered life. It is to "purge our conscience from dead works that we may henceforth serve the living God." It is to convey to us by a vivid symbol what Jesus has pictured by as vivid a parable : " When the Father saw his returning son he ran to him and fell on his neck and kissed him ; and he cried, Put upon him the best robe, and shoes on his feet, and a ring upon his hand; for this my son *was dead, but is alive again !* "

And most assuredly is this the only method of our becoming alive to God; this assurance that God is alive to us. The voice of the moralist is, " Overcome sin, and so make your peace with God." The voice of St. Paul is, " Throw yourself on God as having made peace with you, and so shall you overcome sin." And this is the voice of that baptismal service which has so fully drunk into the spirit of St. Paul.

That teaches you to believe, "I am no longer a child of wrath, but a child of grace; transferred from the world of sense into the world of spirit, that thenceforth all carnal affections may die in me, and all things belonging to the spirit may live and grow in me." And in proportion to this faith,—as it becomes to you no dead formula, but a living principle,—you will "have power and strength to get victory and to triumph against the devil, the world, and the flesh." For you will turn round on the tyrant Sin, to tell him boldly, "I am no longer your servant, but the servant of the living God! I have been bought with a price into the household of a new Master. I have been rescued from the bondage of your Egypt, to be numbered with the children of God's covenant, marching towards the Canaan of God's inheritance!" And thus shall "the joy of the Lord be your strength." And you shall realize the experience of Augustine, "It is one thing to see the land of peace at a distance, with no power to reach it. Quite another to have the road opened out to us by a Divine Leader who can bear and carry us through this road, even to the end. All my bones, then, shall cry, Lord, who is like unto Thee? for *Thou hast broken my bonds in sunder!*"

CHAPTER VIII.

LIFE FOR RIGHTEOUSNESS.

VIII.

THE one great subject kept in view by Paul throughout this important section of his letter to the Roman Christians, from chapter six to chapter eight, is the moral Law of God.

Of his own relation to this Law he first describes the stage of Security, through insensibility to its claims; next that of Struggle, through the opposition of his sinful nature to all endeavour to fulfil these claims; and then the stage of Superiority to this opposing sinfulness, through that new sense of hope, freedom, life, and power which was infused into him by Christ. In no case is the Law of God lost out of sight, in no case its authority lessened, in no case its claim avoided, in no case its eternal necessity in the slightest degree invalidated. The only difference noted is that promised by the Prophets as the grand characteristic of the times of Messiah, the transcription of this Law from the tablets of stone, in which it stood out before men as a national code of statutes, into the fleshy tablets of the heart as a summary of the leading principles of our moral duty towards God and towards men. "This," says Jeremiah, "shall be the covenant that I will make with the house of Israel in the days of the Messiah; I will put my law in their inward parts, and write it in their hearts" (Jer. xxxi. 33).

This, further, is the only difference recognised by Jesus, when he replied to the young ruler who asked him, "What must I do to obtain eternal life?" "Do!" answered our Divine Master, "you know already what you must do. You have been taught it from your youth. You have been consecrated to it in your opening manhood as a 'son of the Law;' you already know the commandments, and you know the promise annexed to them, 'He that doeth these things shall live,' *i.e.*, shall enter into the eternal life which you are longing for. Well then, my answer is in strict accordance with all this: If thou desirest to enter into life, keep the commandments" (Matt. xix. 17)* There can be no other honest interpretation of the words of Jesus than this. The grammar requires it. The context requires it. The serious and not mocking tone of Jesus requires it. The complacent love pervading the mind of Jesus for this earnest seeker after life requires it. And it is confirmed by all the other sayings of our Lord on this point. Look at the Sermon on the Mount. There were some who longed for the times of the Messiah as times of unhallowed freedom (for the world has no notion of liberty but as liberty to do what we please); and how does Jesus meet such? "Never delude yourselves with thinking I am come to do away the Law of God; I am not come to relax its rule,

---

* The unworthy perversion, by some, of our Lord's loving counsel into cruel sarcasm is as bad as Luther's argument against Free-will : " When Moses says, ' Do right,' he means to convince us by practical experience that we *cannot* do right."

but to make this rule more stringent; to bind it on the conscience as well as the conduct, to enthrone it in the moral judgment, and win for it the moral affections. For while the straitest sect of our religion, that of the Scribes and Pharisees, would be satisfied with keeping this Law in the letter of its enactments, I demand that you keep it in the spirit of its principles. Where the letter says merely, 'Thou shalt not kill,' there I say, 'Thou shalt not indulge that angry disposition of which killing words and killing deeds are but the outburst.' Where the letter says simply, 'Thou shalt not commit adultery,' I say, 'Thou shalt not indulge those impure desires which are already adulterous in your heart!' And in all things I declare, 'Except your righteousness, instead of now becoming less rigid, be far more rigid than the righteousness of the Scribes and Pharisees,—except it be transformed from outward doings to inward dispositions, from legal precepts to moral principles,—ye shall by no means enter into the kingdom of heaven,—be counted subjects of it now, or heirs of its bliss hereafter.' Woe therefore to all mistaken teachers who insinuate any relaxation of God's Law! For though they steal about among you seemingly innocent as sheep, you will find them really destructive as wolves. For every one (whether teacher or taught) who fancies himself safe by faith in me as his Lord, instead of by obedience to my Father as his King, can never be received into the kingdom of heaven. He may boast of gifts and of graces of various kinds, but still my final word to him will be, Depart from my presence! You are none of mine, you worker of unrighteousness" (Matt. v. 17-20; vii. 15-23).

The Law, then, instead of being weakened, or made less necessary, under the new Covenant in Christ, is simply summed up into its essential moral principles, and made to reign not merely over outward doings but inward dispositions. Whence our Lord tells the Jewish lawyer (Matt. xxii. 37-40), "Love God, love your neighbour: for on these two commandments hang all the Law and the prophets." And Paul tells the

Galatians who were hankering after their old system, "If you are so anxious to be under Law, remember that all Law is summed up in this, 'Thou shalt love thy neighbour as thyself'" (Gal. v. 14). And he assures the Romans (xiii 9, 10), "All the commandments are briefly comprehended in this saying, Thou shalt love thy neighbour as thyself. For love worketh no sort of injury to our neighbour, therefore love fulfils the Law."

But what, then, is the work of Christ with reference to this unchangeable moral Law? It is just the supply of power to keep this Law. It is just, what Cyprian confirmed by his own experience, "the so forming us, by a second birth, into new creatures, that what was doubted becomes certain, what was closed becomes opened, what was difficult becomes easy, what had seemed impossible becomes within our power." The demand of Jesus is the same as the demand of Moses, only Moses had nothing to say but "Do right," while Jesus has something more; Moses could not pacify the conscience oppressed with the guilt of doing wrong (Heb. ix. 9), while Jesus can; Moses could not breathe into his followers God's Spirit to make their labour not in vain, while Jesus can. "The very thing," says St. Paul, "which the Law could not accomplish, because of the greater strength of our rebellious evil nature, this one thing God accomplishes by having sent His Son to die for us; for he so inflicted the penalty of the Law, which is death, upon Christ's body, that the promise of the Law, which is life, might be freely given to us, provided we walk no longer after the flesh, but after the Spirit" (Rom. viii. 1-4).

Whence you perceive that Paul is no favourer of a feeble, fluctuating, un-moral piety finding for itself a type and an excuse in the helpless struggles of the unconverted wrestler pictured in the seventh chapter. If that were a type of Christian experience, the eighth chapter would be superfluous, nay contradictory. If we find our life exclusively or mainly depicted in that, St. Paul's reproof to the Galatians is too applicable to us: "Christ has become of no effect to you; ye are fallen from grace." And when, alas! we bear too great a resemblance to that chapter, this should be to us a proof not (as some have actually dared to make it) of our piety, but of our lack of piety. For it is not christian, but *un*christian, to find "the law in our members bringing us into captivity to sin." The Christian, on the contrary, "keeps under his body, and brings *that* into subjection." It is *un*christian to be groaning, "O wretched man that I am!" for the Christian declares, "Our rejoicing is this, the testimony of our conscience, that by *the grace of God* we behave ourselves in the world." It is *un*christian to complain, "How to perform that which is good I know not;" for the Christian testifies, "I can do all things through Christ strengthening me." "We have, indeed, no sufficiency in ourselves, but we have sufficiency in God!"

Yet neither, on the other hand, is St. Paul a proud Perfectionist; regarding the Christian as at once complete in all the work he has to do.

He does not look upon himself, or on his brethren, as having attained or being already perfect, but simply as entered afresh for the heavenly race, freed from the despair which before had clogged his every step, and endowed with a new gift of heavenly life, to lay hold at last on the prize for which Christ has laid hold of him. The doctrine of Perfectionism has arisen from a mistaken view of those words in Rom. viii. 2, "The law of the Spirit brought in by Christ Jesus has set me free from the law of sin." For this does not mean " I have become henceforth exempt from sin," but it means, "The new law (or covenant) in Christ, which supplies the Spirit who leads on to life, has broken for me the bonds of the old Law (or covenant) of Moses, which led to death.* The context permits no other interpretation. For as "the Law" in ver. 3 is plainly the Law of Moses, so "the Law"

---

* So Methodius interprets this verse : "The law of the Spirit means the Gospel dispensation." And Semler : " The new law established in Christ, which supplies the Spirit, has freed me from the old law which multiplied sins in me." And Macknight.

in ver. 2, to which this refers as its antecedent, must mean the Law of Moses; and hence, "the law of the Spirit" which is contrasted with it must mean the law (or dispensation) of Christ, which brings in this Spirit.* Besides, ver. 2 is a return to chapter vii. 6, after the long digression in vii. 7-24, and is a reassertion of the statement there, and it consequently means just the same as that statement: "We are *now*, through dying with Christ, set free from the jurisdiction of the old Law of statute obligation, to begin a new life under a new law of spiritual spontaneity." Precisely as Paul says in Galatians v. 24, "They who are Christ's *have crucified* the flesh" (have through their union with Christ made dead the flesh, as much as Christ upon the cross was made dead to the world), that we may henceforth live not in this lower region of the animal nature, but in the higher one, to which Christ

---

* Comp. the meaning of "Law" in Rom. iii. 27: "All boasting is excluded. By what law?" (under what rule, covenant, dispensation?) "that which requires works?" (the law of Moses), "or that which inspires Faith?" (the Law of Christ).

has raised us with himself, of the spiritual world. Which is so far from affirming that the conflict with sin is thenceforth over, or the perfection of the Christian is already complete, that on this new state is grounded the immediately following exhortation to a new battle against sin in correspondence with this state; " If, then, we have thus been crucified as to the flesh, and made alive in Christ in the new world of Spirit, *let us therefore* walk according to this new Spirit!" Exactly as the apostle repeats the exhortation to new conduct grounded on the new position into which we have been raised by Christ, in Colossians ii. 14—iii. 1, "God has blotted out the indictment made against us by the broken ordinances of the Law of Moses, having nailed this indictment, like a bill discharged, to his cross; in order that being now raised up with Christ above those ordinances of the Law of Moses, we may henceforth be occupied with things that are above." The new position of the Christian, therefore, is like that of a bankrupt, for whom his liabilities have been met, and who is set up with new capital, in a new partnership, to make a new start, in a new world. God interests himself for his client's future righteousness. God frees him from the obligations of the past that he may henceforth labour, unencumbered with any liabilities, at this righteousness. God supplies power for this righteousness by a special grant of his own Spirit from himself. What the old *régime* of Moses could not furnish, this is supplied to us in Christ Jesus,—"the *régime of the Spirit*" to empower us for so rising above our lower nature, so beating down this lower nature under our feet, that the blessing promised by the Law may at last become ours; and "as sin has before reigned in us unto death, now grace may reign through righteousness unto eternal life by Jesus Christ our Lord." "It must be *something of heaven* in our mind that shall resist the devil and hell. Open thou thy window and let in the beams of the divine light; then shalt thou find the shadows of the night dispelled, and the warm breath of love transforming thee from darkness to light, from the similitude of Satan into the divine image." *

Now this "something of heaven" which forms the distinctive gift and glory of the new "Law" or dispensation inaugurated by Christ, St. Paul calls, by various phrases, "the Spirit," "the Spirit of Christ," "the Spirit of him who raised up Christ from the dead," and "the Spirit of God dwelling in us."

But "Spirit," we know, means breath; and then, since breath is the concomitant and proof of life, it means emphatically *life*. The Psalmist says to God, "When thou takest away their *breath* they die, but when thou sendest forth thy *Spirit* they are made alive" (Psalm civ. 29). Whence the Nicene Creed distinguishes the Spirit as "the Lord, the giver of *life*."

And the fact that *power* of all kinds varies according to the intensity of life, we know from observation and experience. The more vitality, the more strength; and the draughts on this vitality made by feverish exaltation

* John Smith.

bring out with them unthought-of and immeasurable energies. The somnambulist can accomplish feats which in his ordinary state he would not dare even to think of. The frenzied man exhibits a corporeal strength that overpowers the united force of many of his fellows. Dr. Willis tells us of a patient in whom all the powers of his nature were so intensified that "he eagerly looked forward to the recurrence of his fits, because in them he enjoyed the inrush of thought, imagination, memory, rhythm, music, eloquence, in a continuous stream." And every one knows the testimony of Scripture to the exaltation of men's natural gifts through the inrush of the Spirit of God. As in Moses, of the gift of administrative wisdom, when "the Lord came down and talked with him, and put his Spirit upon him, that he might bear the burden of ruling his people" (Numb. xi. 17); in Gideon, of the gift of martial valour, when "the Spirit of the Lord came upon him, and God saved Israel by his hand" (Judges vi. 34-36); in Samson, of the gift of bodily strength, when "the Spirit of the Lord" began to stir in him, and "came so mightily upon him that he rent the lion as he would have rent a kid" (Judges xiii. 25, xiv. 6); in Micah, the exaltation of the gift of moral boldness, when he could declare, "I am full of power by the Spirit of the Lord, and of judgment and of might, to make clear to Jacob his transgression and to Israel his sin" (Micah iii. 8); and in Paul, of the gift of apostolic diligence and success, when he could testify, "I will not dare to speak of any thing but what Christ hath wrought by me, through *the power of the Spirit of God*" (Rom. xv. 19).

Herein lies the new *Life* provided in Christ to empower his people for righteousness. It is his own resurrection life, infused into the soul of the believer by his Spirit. Paul's one direction for our overcoming all the lust of the flesh—all the rebellious workings of our lower nature—is, "Walk in *the Spirit*;" *i.e.*, live habitually as persons raised up out of this lower nature into a higher and divine world; exalted from the sympathies of earth to the sympathies of heaven; made one with that family of God which unites within itself the saints below and the saints above; beholding the eternal on his throne, and walking in the light as he is in the light! After all the insults that have been hurled at what the world calls "enthusiasm," and notwithstanding all the suspicion raised by the excesses of fanaticism against the truth and beauty of this exalted temper, it still remains undeniable that religion, to have any power over us,—to be anything better than a cold assent to dogmas, and a mechanical round of ceremonies, —*must* become what that word enthusiasm essentially means, "a dwelling in God and God in us,"—a life of God in the soul. All the highest minds will tell you this,—will insist upon this. Plato, for instance, says, "The noblest temper can be wrought in us only by means of that rapture out of ourselves which is the special gift of God." Cicero, that "no one ever became great but through the inspiration of God." Seneca, that "we need not lift up our eyes to heaven, nor beg the sacristan to let us whisper into the ears of an image, in order to be heard by God, for God is very near to us; he is with us; he is in us. Within us dwells the Spirit of God. No one can become good without him. No one rise above the ills of fortune without his help. From him flow all exalted and majestic thoughts. He dwells in every righteous man. From him comes down that divine power which makes the mind lofty, healthy, well-balanced, superior to the hopes and fears of life; for such results can flow from nothing short of God." And this inspired state he illustrates, like St. Paul, by comparing it to an anticipative flight from our corporeal prison house. "The day will come which shall release you from the swaddling bands of the body, and bring you out from all companionship with its contaminating touch. Anticipate, then, now, as far as you can, this release. Fly upward in spirit to that incorporeal region which awaits you. Already raise your aspirations to purer and sublimer things." Even Schopenhauer says, "It is only in the region of the Ideal than we can rise to holiness and happiness; for there only, the things around us become nothing, the thoughts within us everything; there only, the inner man is raised up to his proper height, is freed from time, from impulse, from effort, from desire; there only do we become participant of the supremacy and the eternity of Ideal being; there only become dead to our own petty personality and alive to this Ideal." And Holy Scripture tells us, with authority beyond all these, "The righteousness which the Law prescribes but cannot accomplish shall be realized by those who walk not in the flesh, but in the Spirit." And, "If ye, through the Spirit, put to death the deeds of the body, ye shall gain eternal life." For, "Whosoever is imbued with the Spirit, and given up to his inspirations, shall come to life and bliss."

In such a spirit, therefore, will the Christian endeavour to live and breathe. He has been drawn up towards his heavenly Father, and whatsoever is not of the Father he shuns, nay, hates with a perfect hatred. By habitual prayer he rises above the sympathies of a deceitful world. Let temptation, with her much fair speech, solicit his notice,—he will put her from him with a lofty disgust. Let the siren voices of evil custom strive to allure him from the path of right,—he will bind himself firmly to the mast of holy resolution. His eye is not dazzled by the tinsel of vanity, because it is gazing far beyond the shows of earth into the pure serene of heaven. He cannot herd with the base, because he has a patent of nobility from the King of kings. The endless changes of the lower atmosphere affect him not, because he has climbed up to the mount of God, and looks out thence upon a scene of cloudless magnificence. There may be mists and exhalations, there may be thunders and lightnings agitating things beneath him, but, nevertheless,

"Though round his feet the rolling clouds are spread,
Eternal sunshine settles on his head."

Yet such a lofty "enthusiasm," while it raises us above the spirit of the world, will not withdraw us from the duties of the world. Our Lord provided against this when he told his Father, "I pray not that thou shouldest take them out of the world, but that thou shouldest keep them from the evil one who actuates the world." And St. John has explained how to overcome this wicked one: we must not desert our station in the world, but must abstain from "loving the world and the things that are in the world." There is a sense in which the Christian will be the very life of the sphere which he occupies; like salt to preserve it from corruption, like a light in a dark place, holding up prominently the lamp of life. But we can become such life to our sphere only in proportion as we are inhaling that Spirit of God which raises us above this sphere. Then shall we not only tolerate the world, but love it, with compassion for its sinfulness, labour for its conversion, the sacrifice of our own interests for its welfare. Who, in fact, is so thorough a friend of the world as the man whom the world censures, suspects, despises, as not "its own"? Who is there so actuated by "the enthusiasm for humanity" as he who is filled with the enthusiasm of divinity? Who walks so steadily, righteously, lovingly, beneficently, upon earth, as he whose citizenship is in heaven? When Moses was called up into the mount of God, and admitted to the presence of the Holy One, it was in order that he might then and there receive, and from thence bring down, the tablets of God's *Law* to regulate the conduct and promote the peace and happiness of his people in the wilderness. When John was caught up in the Spirit into heaven, and "behold! a throne before him, and One sitting on the throne," it was in order that he might from this exalted region bring down monitions, encouragements, and promises bearing on his readers amidst the storms of earth. And when Isaiah "saw the King in his glory, and heard the voice of the Lord, and had his lips touched by the Seraphim," it was in order that from this dread magnificence of the court of heaven he might come down as God's ambassador to preach repentance, and to promise, and work out, a good time coming to the inhabitants of earth.

Just in like manner is every Christian raised up with his Lord, that he may come down as his master did from this lofty region to promote God's reign on earth. Our life of new religious consciousness is in order to a life of new moral conduct. See this in Gal. v. 24, 25: "They who are Christ's *have crucified* the flesh," have already passed away from their sin-bearing body, as Christ passed away from the world when he died upon the cross; and what then? "If, then, we now are *living in* the spirit," no longer as citizens of this world, but of the heavenly realm, "let us also *walk* in the spirit;" let us conform our *conduct* here below into harmony with that heavenly life, no longer "coveting vain glory," and the empty praise of men, "no longer provoking one another" by contentious claims about earthly precedence, "no longer envying one another;" for those poor insignificant distinctions of place, and privilege, and gifts, which are given, not for man's exaltation, but for God's service not to make the individual great, but the community good. See again Romans vi. 11 : "As Christ became dead to the world, and is now living with God, so consider yourselves also as dead with him to the world, and living with God;" but for what end? with what result? That henceforth you may pass the rest of your days in idle contemplation of divine dreams, like the mystics of Buddhism? in ecstasies of reverie, like the mystics of the cloister? in that falsely called "religious life" which the mystics of the desert sought in flying from the duties of common life? No! by no means! St Paul's conclusion is just the contrary. "*Therefore*," because you are raised into communion with the immortal spirits, "*therefore* let sin no longer reign in your *mortal body*, by which you are still connected with your fellow-men, but make use of your earthly members as instruments for working out righteousness agreeably to the will of God." And see again Col. iii. 1-11: "Ye are as dead, and your life is hidden with Christ in God;" ye have passed away from the plane of body, into the plane of spirit, as if you had soared into the cloud which encircled Christ's ascension, and were thenceforth hidden with him from the eyes of men; but what then? Are you therefore to doze in personal enjoyment in this cloudland, like a Hindoo Bonze, superior to all the actualities of human life? Nay, but, "*therefore*, wage war with your members which are still on the earth; and *therefore* cultivate kindness, humility, long-suffering with your fellow-men."

> "We need not bid, for cloistered cell,
> Our neighbour and our work farewell,
> Nor strive to wind ourselves too high
> For mortal man beneath the sky;—
> The trivial round, the common task,
> Will furnish all we ought to ask;
> Room to deny ourselves, a road
> To bring us daily nearer God."

CHAPTER IX.

POWER FOR RIGHTEOUSNESS.

IX.

THE sum of what we have been hitherto considering may be stated in the words of St. Augustine: "There is a state of the soul before Law; a state under Law; a state beyond Law." Before Law, when men are living a merely animal or intellectual life, with no sense of relation to God as supreme. Under Law, when we awake to find ourselves subject to a grave responsibility, yet with no power in ourselves to meet the claims upon us. Beyond Law,* when we learn, through Christ, that this Supreme, who is our Lawgiver, is also our Father; and that he who summons us to obedience supplies a spirit of obedience which

* 1 Tim. i. 9, "The Law was not made for a righteous man;" Gal. iii. 11, "The Law was added because of transgressions;" v. 18, " If ye be led of the Spirit, ye are no longer under the Law."

anticipates and surpasses all that the strictest and minutest code of literal statutes can ever lay down. This Spirit comes through faith in Christ as our atonement for the past, and our life for the time to come. And whereas "before Law" (to quote St. Augustine again) "we followed freely our own devices and desires; and under Law were dragged on slavishly by these devices and desires; beyond Law we neither follow them spontaneously, nor are dragged by them reluctantly, but rise up in spirit and in power superior to them all."

All salvation, therefore, turns on our becoming "in the Spirit." The one redemptive force is the life of Christ, which is the life of God, in our soul. All other methods of righteousness fall short of their end. Moral suasion, moral rules, moral stimulants, moral efforts can never, of themselves alone, work out a moral character. It is mockery for men to put us off with treatises on the moral sentiments, volumes on moral casuistry, minute directions for the course in which righteousness should flow, while they leave unanswered the essential preliminary question, Where lies the *well-spring* of righteousness? How shall we open out its crystal streams? Bishop Butler long ago warned us that "going over the theory of virtue in one's thoughts, talking well, and drawing fine pictures of it, this is so far from conducing to form a habit of it in us that it may harden the mind in a contrary course, and render us gradually more insensible to moral considerations." Yet what is this to that still worse mockery which elaborates materialistic theories about the evolution of moral tendencies from ancestral agglomerations, and about moral force stored up in different tissues of the brain, like latent electricity, waiting for the touch which shall release it into active work! The very heathen have seen further than all this. The very proudest sect of ancient moralists tells us that "only by living a divine life, in communion with the gods, can the spirit within us, inbreathed by God as our guide, be enabled to fulfil its work. In all things, therefore, must we pray for the help of God; for thus alone can we fulfil our duty to man."

Now we saw in the preceding chapter that this help from God comes down to the Christian through the Spirit of Christ. Nothing now remains but the question how this infused life for righteousness may be brought out into actual power for righteousness day by day.

Here we must remember the well-known principle that Power is proportionate to belief in power. Diffidence leads to cowardice, and thus to impotency; while confidence begets courage, and therewith competency. The Roman poet sings, "They find themselves able because they think themselves able." Locke says, "From discernment of possibility we come by the idea of Power." And always, active *will* springs out from passive *wish* in proportion as we see our way to accomplish this wish.

On this principle, therefore, our Lord continually insists as the root of all-sufficiency, physical and moral. When he found his disciples powerless over evil, his cry of disappointment and reproof is, "*O unbelieving generation, how long shall I bear with you?*" When they ask him, "Why could not we cast out the demon?" he replies more clearly, "Because of your *unbelief*, for if you had *faith*, were it only like a grain of mustard seed, you might remove mountains, and nothing would be impossible to you." And when, as to moral power, they exclaim, "If there must be so much of victory over self, who can be saved?" the answer of Jesus is, "Very true; with merely human wish this is impossible, but with the will derived from power divine all things are possible." And Paul re-echoes his Master when he asks the Galatians, "Received ye the Spirit which works wonders in you, from the doing of Law, or from the faith which comes through hearing about Christ?" And for all the mighty deeds of all saints he has but one explanation, "Through *faith* they subdued kingdoms and wrought our righteousness."

What, then, is this faith which is the root of

all power? It is faith in God's paternity of us, God's presence in us, God's purpose for us.

1. First, the power of the Christian depends upon his faith in *God's paternity of him*. In all things, as Christians, we must be copies of Christ. And we know how such faith in the Fatherhood of God wrought in him all his works. This faith displayed itself in Jesus in early youth: "Where should you look for me but in *my Father's house?*" This faith was confirmed in him at his baptism by the Voice from heaven, "Thou art my beloved Son." This was enjoyed by him through all the vicissitudes of his earthly course. When hopeful, his cry was, "I thank thee, O *Father!*" When troubled, it was, "*Father*, glorify thy name!" And by this he was actuated in all that he said and did: "I do nothing of myself, but only what I see *my Father* do." Nay, even the temporary cloud which overshadowed him on the cross came through no loss of faith in his Father's relation to him, for his cry then was still, "*My* God, *my* God!" but only through loss of com-

prehension of his Father's dealings with him. And from all this we learn that the very first feeling to be cherished by every one who, being in Jesus, partakes of the Spirit of Jesus, is this of childlike confidence in the Fatherhood of God.

Yet nothing is so alien from even the theology, as well as the morality, of the vast majority of men, as this confidence. Nothing is so left out of view in the narrow systems of controversial divinity. Nothing is being so fatally undermined by the materialistic teaching of what is now called science. Men live either "without God" altogether, or with a dim, uneasy sensation that the "Unknowable" is far above, not only out of their sight, but out of all personal relation to them; with no likeness to them, no care for them, no condescension towards them. Whence the great importance of the fact, related by St. Luke, that the very first truth which Paul pressed upon his hearers at Athens was, "God is not far from any one of us; for in him we live and move and have our being, and *we are his offspring,*" *i.e.,* of his race and kin. The apostle evidently counted this as the foundation principle on which alone he could build any hope of winning his hearers to Christ and to God. There were before him Epicureans who denied this truth; who obligingly relieved their gods from the burdensome task of any relation to man, any care of man, any communication with men. And therefore the apostle, with his usual tact, begins with enlisting other of his hearers, the Stoics, upon his side by quoting from their finest teacher the decisive declaration, "We are all God's offspring."

And here he had with him the testimony of all the wisest men who would be reverenced by that motley crowd. The inscription on the temple of Apollo at Delphoi was the first to insist upon this fundamental truth. For that admonition (whether from Chilo or directly from the god), "Know thyself," has not the meaning so often mistakenly assigned to it by modern writers, of "Delve and grub into the recesses of your own minds to discover their composition and their working;" but rather, "Become aware of what you are *in relation to the Supreme;* whence you spring; whose image you bear; with what capacity you are endowed; so that recognizing your divine birth you may live a divine life." This is clearly the sense in which Socrates understands it when he asks Euthydemus, "Have you noticed that inscription on the temple at Delphoi, and tried to learn thence *what sort of being you are;* what capacity has been bestowed on you for acting as a man should act? For whosoever is not aware of this his proper capacity, *knows nothing of himself;* he fails to know his special business in this world; he falls into numberless errors, and misses his proper aim." And just in like manner Plato makes Socrates say to Alcibiades, "When the Delphic oracle enjoins us to know ourselves, it means to *know our soul, what that is;* what that intelligence therein which is *divine,* which we have in common with God, and which makes us similar to God." Which meaning is still more insisted on by Cicero when he says, "To know one's self is to know one's soul. For unless there were a something *divine* in us, such a precept would not have been accounted so superhuman as to come from God. He, therefore, who knows himself, will know his intellect to be an image dedicated to the Deity; and in the spirit of such a gift from God, will ever think and act in a manner worthy thereof. He will be sensible with what capacity he has been sent into the world, with what powers endowed for the making of himself a good, and thus a happy man." The sum and substance, therefore, of this precept is given by Antoninus when he says, "Bear always in mind what is your proper nature, and what a wondrous part you are of him who dwells and rules in all things, from whom you flow as does a stream from its parent fountain." And the practical bearing of this precept is insisted on by Epictetus when he urges, "If we would but thus remember how we spring from God, in such a way as no other earthly creature does, we surely never could indulge any thoughts or deeds unworthy of God. What if Cæsar had adopted you into his family? How elated would you thenceforth be! And shall not then your being of the family of *God* rouse up your spirit to its proper height? Alas! that so many should rather incline towards their relationship with brutes than their relationship with God!"

And I need remind no student of his Bible how constantly this first principle of all divine life is taught us in Holy Scripture. This begins at the beginning with the amazing disclosure that man is made in the image of God. This tells us that, notwithstanding all our degeneracy, this image remains as the distinctive feature and prerogative of man. Nay, this discloses to us that the one end of the revelation of the Father through His Son is to wake us up to the recognition and belief of this high lineage, and to make us anew in consciousness what we were at first made in idea, the sons of God. And it annexes to this belief just the practical results which flow from it alone, of moral superiority to our earthly nature, and moral culture of our heavenly nature. "Behold," says John, "what marvellous love the Father has bestowed on us, that we should be hailed by him as sons of God!" And what follows from such an experience? "Whosoever is thus begotten into consciousness of sonship with God, can never commit sin, which is contrariety to God. For the divine seed which has begotten him remains within him, making sin abominable to him, as one begotten of God" (1 John iii. 1-9); that is, just so much and so long as we realize our heavenly relationship, we cannot stoop to earthly inconsistencies with this relationship, any more than the rosebud can blossom into henbane, or the sweet fountain throw out bitter waters. Whence Paul says to the Ephesians, "Being God's dear children, be ye *therefore*" (as the proper consequence) "imitators of your Father!" And Peter, "Since ye have waked up to call God your Father, be ye holy as he is holy." And our Lord himself, "Labour after a perfection, not like that of Scribes and Pharisees, but reflecting the perfection of your Father in heaven."

See this essential connection between faith in God's fatherly relation to us, and self-surrender to his fatherly authority over us, in our Master's picture of the Prodigal Son. It was failure of filial feeling which led him down to ruin. It was recovery of filial feeling which redeemed him out of ruin. From the first he had a father, and to the last continued to have a father; but he was not at one with that father; he had no confidence in that father's wisdom and love; he was drawn aside to tastes, and interests, and pursuits at war with that father. Hence his desire to get away from this father's presence, to break off the last link of dependence on this father's authority; to set up for himself, on his own resources; to do his own will, and make his own life, in entire separation from his father. His plea is, "I have now grown out of infancy into manhood; I have risen from a subordinate, dependent state, to have a right to be my own master. Give me what I can justly claim, the portion of goods that is due to me!" And thereupon he departs from his father (which is the first step in all sin); takes his journey into a far country, out of reach of his father's interference; and there wastes his substance in what he no doubt called self-possession and self-enjoyment, but what Jesus calls "self-abandonment." No longer recognizing his relationship as son, he no longer cherishes any of the feelings, sympathies, dispositions, actions of a son. Though the relationship remained and could not be dissolved, his sense of this relationship was utterly laid to sleep. But mark what our Lord depicts as the very first symptom of incipient recovery. It is not disappointment, it is not wretchedness, it is not starvation,—it is the rising once again into his consciousness of the thought and of the name of his *father*. "When he came to himself" (was waking out of his mad fit) "he said, How many hired servants of *my father's* have bread enough and to spare! I will arise, and go back to this *father!*" Before, in his growing self-will, he had thought of the author of his life only as his superior, his "governor," his unwelcome controller, whom he could not go along with, and must therefore run away from. But now, he thinks of him as his sole remaining *refuge;* as bearing to him a relationship which could never be effaced, and to which all the intervening temporary partnerships of vice and folly were but as a passing dream. "All others have disappointed me! All others have been untrue to me! All others have wrought me ruin! All others have forsaken me in this ruin! Of all others, 'no man giveth unto me!' Where then is the one link left unbroken? Where my last resort? My father! I will arise, and go back to my father!"

In like manner is the essence of all conversion in every man a return to God as our Father; a recollection, recognition, laying hold, of that one relation which can never be utterly broken off between the creature and his Creator,—the son, made in his Father's image, and this Father himself. In one stage of our experience, truly, this relation is mere emptiness, or if recognised becomes a burden and a terror. We seek to escape from the very notion of it. We fancy it "liberty" to be relieved from all belief in it. We get as far as possible from books and persons and ordinances which remind us of "religion," *i.e.*, a being *bound* in any way to this Supreme One. But when our dream of independence is clogged with nightmare, or broken up by rude hands; when our delirium has run its course, and we "come to ourselves," then, most assuredly, there is nothing but this relationship which we have so obstinately disbelieved that can preserve us from despair. It may seem quite new to us. It may be represented as impossible. We may be tempted to doubt our parentage, and think of ourselves as sons of Satan, rather than of God. But *still this alone will save us.* This alone will put into our hearts the thought, and hope, and power, "I will arise" and flee from all my miseries and sins. What! is God "not far from me"? "Do I in him live and move and have my being?"

Am I "his offspring"? Does he "hold me by my right hand"? Is he "guiding me by his counsel, and intending me for his glory"? Oh then to "arise and go to him!" Oh to cry out, in my utter destitution, "Whom have I in heaven but thee? who upon earth in comparison with thee?" Oh to hope, though with the faintest faith, that notwithstanding my self-debasement, my self-reproach, my wretchedness, my rags, there may be something in his bosom still of fatherly compassion towards me! Yes, "Father," "*my* Father!"—this must be for me the turning-point, this my only possible cry! Though I have so long gone away from thee,—yea, *because* departing from thee I have found nothing but ruin, let me plead the relationship which *thou* hast not forgotten! Let me once more see thy face! Take me back, even to the lowest office in thy service,—even to be only a serf and slave! Henceforth I will have no will but thine, no interest but thine, no occupation but to please thee, no life but a life of entire self-surrender to thee."

And what, think you, was the result? When the father so graciously acknowledged the relationship which constituted the prodigal's only plea; when he ran to meet him, threw around him a father's arms, gave him a father's kiss, clothed him with every symbol of entire restoration to all the privileges of sonship,—would not this recovered son, think you, go forth from the banquet of welcome, to do a son's work in his father's household, with a son's spirit of loyalty, with a son's conscientiousness, diligence, perseverance, such as no hirelings ever can attain to; with a son's sympathy for all his father's plans, and interests, and demands? Assuredly yes! For this returned son's will was now in as perfect accordance with his father's will as the planet which glides, by its own centripetal spontaneity, along the path marked out for it, around its parent Sun! And so his whole life declares, "As my father giveth me commandment, even so I do!"

2. But all moral power depends, in the second place, on *faith in God's presence in us.* For the

thought of God's relation to us is only of an objective fact. There is needed something more *subjective* than this; a personal experience corresponding with this fact; an inward life flowing into us from this fact. Of that returned son in the parable it might be figuratively said that the spirit of his father thenceforth dwelt in him and actuated him; he thought, and felt, and did as his father would have him think, and feel, and do. But our experiences of the religious life must be something more than figurative. As this life is derived from God, it can be kept up in us only as God himself dwells in us. Just as in nature the Living One is the perpetual life of all lives, warming in the sun, refreshing in the breeze, glowing in the stars, and blossoming in the trees, and *living through all life;* so, in the human soul, the Father of spirits is the breath of our spirit, and on our personal communion with this breath in us depends the vitality of our intellectual, moral, and spiritual existence. Whatever in us constitutes the distinct humanity of our nature has its source in fountains higher than itself. As surely as the brook, which sparkles through the clods of earth, and brings out from them flowers and fruits, is not of these clods, but is fed by infiltrations from the heavens, so surely does each rill of truth, and beauty, and sanctity which percolates through our mind give evidence of a spiritual, supernatural origin. It shows itself to be "the breath of the power of God, and a pure influence from the glory of the Almighty." The truths which flash upon the man of science he recognises as not excogitated by him, but unveiled to him; he does not make them, he simply finds them. The forms of beauty in painting and sculpture are no products of the artist's caprice, but models for his imitation. The concords of harmony do not rise out of us, they descend upon us. When men broke out in admiration of Mozart he burst into tears, exclaiming, "Not mine! not mine! It has been given me!" And the avowal of Coleridge is that of every poet

> "I may not hope from outward forms to win
> The passion and the life whose fountain is within!"

And just so is it with the perception, the love, and the enthusiasm of the spiritual man for all the pure ideas of moral beauty and moral harmony. We behold them rising on the mind like the morning dawn. We acknowledge them as "the fountain light of all our day, the master light of all our seeing," and as "truths which wake, to perish never." We bow before them as the planet rulers of our life. We worship them as guides from earth to heaven. And we count the one end of our being and becoming to be the diligent transformation of ourselves into their image and likeness. And just in proportion as we thus feel ourselves not possessing these inspirations from on high, but rather possessed by them, do they exert on us a power to mould our whole demeanour and character into this likeness. Every earnest Christian feels with humble adoration, "Not my own, but all of grace! Not the work of man, but the gift of God!" and in this very feeling rises to the height of his high calling; is quickened and empowered to comport himself as a vessel unto honour, set apart and meet for the Master's use! So it was with Jesus, the Great Exemplar. When the contemptuous Scribes cried, "How can this Man teach, who has had no training in our schools?" the answer of the Son of God was, "My teaching comes not from myself, but from the Father who has sent me. I think the thoughts he puts into my mind. I speak the words he puts into my mouth. And hence it is that every heart which is attuned into unison with my Father's will finds in these words and thoughts a melody kindred with his own, which stirs into responsiveness every chord within him!" Thus it was that Jesus was "the realized possibility of life in God."* His thoughts, his feelings, his desires, his plans, were regulated by the Spirit of his Father dwelling in him, as the hands of a watch, down even to seconds, are regulated by the mainspring within.

* Martineau.

And this Spirit which thus possessed the Son of God he promises to impart to all his brethren. "If ye hold fast what I have taught you concerning the Father and his relation to you, the Spirit of the Father, which you have seen daily, dwelling in me, shall in like manner dwell in you. And then shall you know by your own experience how the Father himself can come to you and take up his abode with you." And this experience St. Paul assumes to be in all who are members of Christ: "Ye are a holy temple of the Lord, builded together for a dwelling-place of God, through the Spirit." And on this experience he builds his expectations of their moral purity and goodness: "Ye are the temple of the living God, as he promised, for the distinctive mark of his new dispensation and new method of righteousness, I will dwell in them, and walk in them. *Therefore* cleanse yourselves from all filthiness of flesh and spirit, perfecting holiness, in the fear of God!"

Yet how seldom does this indwelling of the

Spirit of God in us seem to be considered indispensable to all moral excellence! You may turn over volume after volume of dreary ethical disquisitions, and find, amidst the clearest classification of duties, almost nothing about *how* these duties are to be accomplished. The upshot of their practical suggestions is simply, "Heal thyself!" The only counsel for the taming of the passions is like the physician's advice to poor Queen Mary:

> " He says,
> That rest is all—tells me I must not think ;—
> That I must rest! . . . .
> Catch the wild cat, cage him, and when he springs
> And maims himself against the bars, say Rest."

Not like Jesus, who first tamed the writhing demoniac by casting out the devil that possessed him; who first healed the thirty years' cripple, and put new life into him, and then said, when he had made him whole, "Sin no more!" True, indeed, that the subsidiary means of our recovery from sin are a conscience enlightened by moral instruction; a taste made sensitive to moral distinctions; a will aroused to action by vivid pictures of the wretchedness of sin, the bliss of righteousness; a habit of virtue gained by self-inspection and self-culture; but all these are only as the enumeration of the parts and functions of a steam-engine, with no indication of the source whence must proceed its motive-power. All these may help to chisel and polish the surface of the statue we are endeavouring to shape; they bring not with them the spark from heaven which shall give this statue life. This spark must come to us from the Son of God; must be fanned into flame by the Spirit of God; must kindle in us hope, and power, and patience in all our conflicts with sin, through the stirring consciousness of God's indwelling in our inner man. "What?" says the religious philosopher, "do you count it impossible for man to ascend to God? Nay, but God himself descends to you; yea, rather, with still closer intimacy, takes up his abode *within* you. For no one is made good but through the indwelling of God."

And would you have a vivid presentment, even to your very senses, of the moral power of such a consciousness of God in us, gaze at that noble picture of "Diana or Christ." See how the delicate, feeble girl is being raised out of herself and her position, with no ear and no eye for the quivering crowds around her, nay with no heart for the agonizing looks of the lover close to her. "Her eyes are homes of silent prayer." She is filled with one single image, sensible of one single Presence, gazing into one single countenance, which eclipses all things else:—

> "She sees a hand they cannot see,
> Which beckons her away:
> She hears a voice they cannot hear,
> Which says she must not stay!"

And hence you behold her calm in the midst of confusion, passionless in the midst of passion. No struggle with the blandishments of temptation, but simply a soaring above them; no resistance to the whispers of affection, but simply a being rapt beyond them. Not a muscle contracted, not a nerve quivering, not a look drawn aside, not a feature agitated, not a tear falling, but simply a divine composure enfolding her like the gentle breath of eve. Self-possessed because possessed by God; immovable by man because at rest in God; dead to the world because alive unto God! Instinctively we "fall down on our face, confessing that *God is in her of a truth.*"

3. But there is one thing more, through which (and which alone) the power that we need for overcoming sin can fill our souls,—faith, namely, not merely in God's paternity of us, and his presence in us, but, moreover, *in his purpose for us.*

Nothing is more certain than the fundamental principle of all Theism—that purpose reigns throughout the universe.* This principle is the necessary deduction from the *facts* with which we are acquainted of this universe; down from the revolutions of the heavenly bodies to the minutest changes in microscopic

* See my "A B C of Philosophy," 78-94.

life. And this principle guarantees to us that for every creature in this universe there is a destiny pre-determined in God's purpose, and being carried out, notwithstanding any amount of seeming contradiction or delay, by God's providence. In the light of this principle, therefore, we must contemplate God's dealings not only in nature, but in grace; not only with all inferior things, but with the highest of his earthly creatures, man. Man, also, God has made according to a pre-existent Ideal, in order to bring him, through whatever length of intermediate education and discipline, to the realization of this Ideal. We are made after the divine Image, in order to become partakers of the divine nature. This is our destiny as men, the ultimate frustration of which would be a frustration of all that makes God to be God,— his wisdom, his goodness, his power. Therefore, through whatsoever vicissitudes of experience, external or internal, we are obliged to pass, and to whatsoever delay in the making of us we may be subjected, this is *the end* for which our heavenly Father, having first given us life, will go on to continue in us life, and to develope in us life till it be reached.

And the Christian becomes awake to the belief of this his princely destiny. He learns with certainty, through the teaching of his Master, that he is akin to God. He experiences, with additional certainty, through the incoming of his Master's Spirit, that he is made the habitation of God. And he draws from these two incontrovertible premisses—the premiss of doctrine as taught him by Christ, and the premiss of fact as wrought in him by the Spirit of Christ—the equally incontrovertible conclusion, *Therefore* my Father will certainly accomplish that end for which he made me, has redeemed me, and is sanctifying me. For this Father is not only "he that is, and that was, and that is to come," with no variableness or shadow of change; but also "the Alpha and Omega, the beginning and the ending" of all things. Every series, therefore, which he has begun, with the first letter, he will complete even to the last letter. And as the last letter for all the works of God is their being brought by successive increments up to the perfect integration of their nature; their being raised to the highest power of this nature; their being rounded off to that completeness, in view of which God made them at all; so the last letter for his human family is their being invested with the full-robed righteousness for which God has from the first intended them.

And on this principle of God's *faithfulness* to the end which he has designed for us, St. Peter bases all his demands on us to escape from corruption and to abound in holiness. "There are given to us exceeding great and precious promises, that *by these*"—through the life and power which they convey into the soul—"you may come to be participant of the divine nature." St. John, in like manner, bases all his demand for purity on this belief in privilege: "Now are we the sons of God, and we know that we are destined to partake of his glory; and if so, surely every one hoping to share the glory of God will now, beforehand and at once, endeavour to purify himself into some share of the character of God." Which is just the principle whereby St. Paul throws life and power into the Roman Christians, as the closing thought in the passage we have been dwelling on: "Ye have received no longer a spirit of bondage, causing fear of God; but the spirit of sonship, which cries to him, Abba, Father; and if thus we are sealed as sons, this shows that we are also heirs; heirs of God as much as Christ is heir!" This life and power constitute that "firstfruit of the Spirit," —*i.e.*, the Spirit as a firstfruit and pledge of more to come,—of which he speaks in viii. 23. This Spirit is as sure a guarantee of our ultimate perfectionment as the first sheaf of corn is of the harvest home. As the apostle repeats in 2 Cor. v. 5: "He has wrought us into fitness for eternal life, and has given us his Spirit as the *earnest* of its final grant to us." As surely as the buyer is bound by his "handsel," or pledge given "in hand," to complete his contract, so surely has God pledged himself by the Spirit already advanced to us to fulfil all his promises to us. Whence Paul reminds the Ephesians, "When you had given Christ your confidence you were sealed" (marked out as his) "with that Holy Spirit, promised to believers, which is the earnest" (or caution money) "of our inheritance; a pledge to us till the time shall come when God shall put us in full possession of the inheritance purchased for us." Whence, again, he tells the Corinthians, that "the Lord will confirm them to the end, to make them blameless in the last day; for God is faithful to his engagements with all who have been called into fellowship with his Son." And he recommends to the Thessalonians, as one effectual source of Christian strength against all enemies, the firm belief that "God has not appointed us to wrath, but to obtain salvation by our Lord Jesus Christ."

And oh the all-sufficiency of this faith in the faithfulness of God to make us strong in the Lord and in the power of his might! We may multiply rules of righteousness, discipline ourselves in acts of righteousness, labour to consolidate habits of righteousness; but for all this we must have a Friend to look up to, a Father to lean upon; his everlasting arms to be our refuge. As a child turns from its own ineffectual efforts to ask its mother's aid, so must we turn continually, in our disappointments and our impotency, to a stronger than ourselves. "God help me!" is a charm to work with, mightier than a thousand personal "I will's." For while everything in ourselves is fluctuating, everything in God is stable. Our prospects may be often overcast; the elements may seem against us; the declining year may bring with it declining strength; but amidst the grey gloom of a weeping atmosphere, and the desolate drip of falling leaves, the eternal love of God makes sure to us the return of spring. Life, we are certain, will follow upon death, and seeds now checked by frost shall come out in full bloom hereafter. For God is with us. He desires our righteousness even more than we. And his purpose must prevail. How beautifully is this simple confidence in the faithfulness of God made the sum and substance of the consolation of his saints in their dying moments. The last words of Wesley were, "The best of all is, God is with us. The Lord of Hosts is with us, the God of Jacob is our refuge!" The last of Francke, "God will support me." Of Jonathan Edwards, "Trust in God, and ye need not fear." Of Dr. Whewell, "The eternal God is my refuge, and underneath are the everlasting arms!" The last of Luther, "Into thy hands I commend my spirit, for thou hast redeemed me, thou God of faithfulness." And herein did he simply echo the last words of his Master, "Father, into thy hands I commend my spirit."

And thus both our life and power for all present service, and our anticipation of all future blessedness, are based upon the bright, well-grounded confidence of the faithfulness of our heavenly Father. We know that he who has begun a good work in us will carry it on till the day of Christ. And therefore, seeing that no one has ever in this world finished his battle with sin, that no one has yet attained the mark of his high calling in Christ, our entrance on another stage of being wherein this goal set before us may be reached, this prize be made over to us, is guaranteed by the faithfulness of him who has promised. Even, therefore, in our deepest trials, when our heart is grieved and our reins are consumed, we may cry, with the Psalmist's faith and hope, "*Nevertheless*, I am still with thee! Thou art holding me by my right hand. Thou art guiding me by thy counsel till thou shalt receive me to thy glory!" Ah truly! "to such as feel in themselves the working of the Spirit of Christ, mortifying the works of the flesh and their earthly members, and drawing up their mind to high and heavenly things, the godly consideration of predestination and our election in Christ is full of sweet, pleasant, and unspeakable comfort, because it doth greatly establish and confirm our faith of eternal salvation."

> "For souls that of God's own good life partake,
> He loves as his own self. Dear as his eye
> They are to him, he'll never them forsake,
> When they shall die, then God himself shall die;
> They live, they live, in blest eternity!" *

* Henry More.

WORKS BY THE SAME AUTHOR.

I.
THE FATHERHOOD OF GOD.
4s. 6d. (*Hatchard.*)

"One of the most lucid and forcible expositions of the paternal character of God. It displays the stores of a well-furnished and a well-balanced mind."—*Quiver.*

II.
SERMONS FOR THE TIMES
AT ST. PAUL'S CATHEDRAL.
6s. (*Longmans.*)

"Very vigorous and original. A cultured scholarship pervades them."—*British Quarterly.*

"Will tend to confirm the reputation he has won as a philosophical thinker."—*Inquirer.*

"Of very great excellence. Mr. Griffith is a scholar, a man of extended information, and a divine."—*Church Herald.*

III.
THE A B C OF PHILOSOPHY.
5s. (*Longmans.*)

"Mr. Griffith is a writer whom we always welcome. He is one of that small company who have not despaired of philosophy, and who hope that faith and philosophy may yet shake hands."—*Literary World.*

"One of the many contributions of that remarkable writer to philosophical thought."—*The Principal of Wycliffe Hall, Oxford.*

IV.
THE GOSPEL OF THE DIVINE LIFE.
A STUDY OF THE FOURTH EVANGELIST.
14s. (*Kegan Paul & Co.*)

"Deserves careful study. Few books of greater significance have appeared for many years."—*Edinburgh Review.*

"The whole book is full of power, labour, and masterly exposition."—*English Churchman.*

www.ingramcontent.com/pod-product-compliance
Lightning Source LLC
Chambersburg PA
CBHW020919230426
43666CB00008B/1500